The Fight

For

Light

The Spiritual Battle With Chronic Illness

Robert T. Murphy B.D.

A story of the lives of a Christian who is a chronic liver disease patient and his dear wife. How God, family, and friends carried us through.

P.O.Box 464
Miamitown, OH 45041
www.daystarpublishing.org

All Scripture is from the Authorized King James Holy
Bible; God's only word.

*"The entrance of thy words giveth light; it giveth
understanding unto the simple."*

Ps 119:130

Reprinted by permission. (A Bend In The Road), Dr. David Jeremiah,
2000, Thomas Nelson Inc. Nashville, Tennessee. All rights reserved.

ISBN 978-1-890120-87-0
Library of Congress 2012954805

In Appreciation

To my wife, Pam. After thirty-six years of marriage, staying with me through "better and worse," no man could possibly have had a better life's companion. Your love has sustained me through all the heartaches, failures, and victories of our lives together. I only hope that I have been as good a husband to you as you have been a wife to me.

Pr 12:4a "A virtuous woman is a crown to her husband... I love you and always will!

To my sons and their wives for your concern, support, help, and easily felt love. No man has ever had better sons and daughters-in-law. May God bless you every day of your lives!

To my In-Laws, who certainly don't fit into the typical In-Law joke category, thank you for all your love and support these many years. You have been a great blessing to Pam and me all our lives.

To my sister and her husband, who came all the way across the country on more than one occasion to visit me. Thank you for all you have done for me and my entire family. It has been a great blessing and fun getting reacquainted again.

To my Pastor, Rick DeMichele, and his wife, Carol. In the darkest hours of our lives you were there for us. Your experiences of suffering with, and caring for, the trials of Leukemia have been invaluable in helping us get through some of the worst days we have ever experienced. Your prayers, friendship, support, and faithfulness have earned our eternal loyalty and respect for you both.

To my church family and all those around the world who have prayed, sent cards, called, and helped us financially: there is no group of people on this earth with whom I would rather be associated; you have truly been a remarkable family.

To the best doctors and nurses in the world, both in Boise and Portland, thank you all for your dedication to your profession, and for your best efforts in keeping me alive. All of you will always have a special place in my heart.

To my disease: thank you for the compassion for others, closeness to the Lord Jesus Christ, appreciation for life, for re-uniting my sister and me, and for the closeness to my family I have enjoyed because of you.

And last, but certainly the most important, to my Savior and personal Friend the Lord Jesus Christ, God manifest in the flesh (1 Timothy 3:16). Without You stepping into my life, saving my soul, and changing my entire life, I would not only not be alive today. I would certainly have taken my place among the damned in Hell a very long time ago. You've made my life a testimony to the love, longsuffering, grace, and mercy of the one true and living God. All glory be to you, the King of Kings and Lord of Lords. I am a trophy of God's grace!

I certainly would not be sitting here writing these words without the contributions of all of you! Thank you all, and I pray God's richest blessings on all of you.

Table of Contents

Introduction

The only time you can get safely off the roller coaster after it starts moving is at the end of the ride. If you quit the ride before then, it will cause pain or death.

Bob Murphy 3/2012

Ps 77:14 "Thou art the God that doest wonders: thou hast declared thy strength among the people."

"I have fought a good fight, I have finished my course, I have kept the faith:"

2 Tim 4:7

Do some of the hospital departments address you by your first name? Have you ever been sick of being sick, and tired of being tired? Have you ever begun to shake at the sight of a syringe or the thought of going to the hospital or doctor? Have you ever looked at a handful of pills and thought, "Oh God, not again?" If you have, then you are most likely part of the world of the chronically ill. I think Charles Dickens put it best when he penned the words "It was the best of times, it was the worst of times... It was the season of Light, it was the season of Darkness..."[1] That quote from his classic book *A Tale of Two Cities* describes very aptly the Christian lives of my wife (Pam) and me in the years 2010-2012. After thirty

---

[1] Charles Dickens, *A Tale of Two Cities,* (Kindle Edition), p. 3.

years of being saved and living the best Christian lives we could, the greatest trial of our faith hit us quite unexpectedly in February of 2011. Do the tests of God ever end? Unfortunately they do not! As long as we are still turning oxygen into carbon dioxide, and *looking* at the daisies instead of *pushing them up*, the trials will continue. Is it worth it to go on, even when there appears to be no hope or reason why we should? Absolutely. That is the reason for this book: not for us to glory in our infirmities for our glory's sake, but to glory in our infirmities for the glory of the Lord Jesus Christ for what He has done for us, and with us, through it all. This is a testimony of *His* grace, growth, peace that passes all understanding, and miracles in our lives. The Apostle Simon Peter tells us:

1 Pet 1:6-8 Wherein ye greatly rejoice, though now for a season, if need be, ye are in heaviness through manifold temptations: {7} That the trial of your faith, being much more precious than of gold that perisheth, though it be tried with fire, might be found unto praise and honour and glory at the appearing of Jesus Christ: {8} Whom having not seen, ye love; in whom, though now ye see him not, yet believing, ye rejoice with joy unspeakable and full of glory...

My hope in writing this book is that it might encourage all who read it to not be afraid of the Lord's trials no matter how severe they may be, or how hopeless they appear. They are orchestrated and sent to us, with all the love in the universe, for the dual purpose of making us better Christians, and for glorifying the Lord.

(Phil 1:6) Being confident of this very thing, that he which hath begun a good work in you will perform it until the day of Jesus Christ.

May God grant you the joy that He has given us through this experience, and prepare you for a profoundly new, and blessed way of Christian living.

Bob Murphy B.D.
March 2012,

Chapter One: My Testimony

The letter was from the American Red Cross, twenty-three years ago, and read something like this:

Dear Mr. Murphy:
This letter is to inform you that you are no longer eligible to donate blood. Tests show that you are a carrier of non-A, non-B Hepatitis, (now designated Hepatitis-C) a contagious disease. We recommend that you see your doctor in the near future to discuss this finding and explore your options. Thank you for your past participation in the blood donation program, and good luck in the future.
Sincerely…

Non-A, non-B Hepatitis? What is that? They didn't even have a real name for it back then, kind of like movie stars whose name we know as whatever Hollywood has decided to name them. What is their real name? Who knows?

A trip to the doctor was about as enlightening as trying to hold a conversation with "Stitch," my dachshund. It entailed lots of head-cocking and puzzled expressions. It went something like this:

Me: So Doctor, exactly what is non-A, non-B Hepatitis?
Doc: We don't exactly know (head cocked).
Me: How did I get it?
Doc: We don't know how anyone gets it.
Me: What is the treatment for it?
Doc: At this time we're not sure (head cocked in other direction).

Me: Is it life threatening?
Doc: Possibly.
Me: How long would you guess I have?
Doc: Perhaps a few years, perhaps you'll die of old age.
Me: What do I do now?
Doc: Have yearly blood tests done and keep an eye on it.

Wow, and I'm actually paying him for this? But please don't think I am against the medical profession. After all these years of dealing with this problem, this past year has brought me a new-found, and tremendous respect, for what the medical profession can accomplish. But you could never have convinced me of that when I left his office that day. In all fairness, however, it was a new type of Hepatitis, and there just wasn't much information available.

After blood tests by a lab in Pensacola, Florida I was told that I had a mild case of Hep-C and that there was nothing to do about it. It was there but wasn't causing any real problems. That was the worst health advice I had ever been given, but the same advice was repeated many times over the next twenty-one years. So nothing was done except for occasional monitoring. Looking back now, I cannot help but think that if they had treated me for the disease back then, I would not be practically incurable now.

Then in the summer of 2008 while doing lawn care work, I started becoming very fatigued and sick. Not knowing what was going on, I weathered the storm the rest of the year. In the summer of 2009, I started having severe nose bleeds, bleeding gums, and wounds which took much longer to stop bleeding than normal. I went to see a Heptologist, and, in September, she sent me for a liver biopsy. It was determined I had fourth stage liver fibrosis; the next step was cirrhosis. I had gone from nothing to almost critical in one year! The doctor said it was an Auto- Immune Hepatitis, in addition to the Hep-C, and started me on massive doses of Prednisone (a strong steroid).

I ended up walking into bookshelves and apologizing to them for doing so! I didn't even realize I had done it until my wife said: Did you just walk into the bookshelf and apologize to it? It was like the old drugs days; I was once again a "Starship Trooper."

In February 2011, I contracted the flu and everything went to pieces. The flu lowered my immune system sufficiently to allow the Hep-C to proliferate. I was taken, by Pam, to the emergency room of the VA Hospital in Boise, Idaho, and went from the E.R. to the hospital's "Step Down" center and was admitted. I was given blood transfusions and blood platelets to stop the bleeding. The doctors did the best they could, and I received excellent care, but not being liver specialists they really had no idea what to do. They contacted the Portland, Oregon, V.A. Medical Center, one of the best liver hospitals in the world. The doctors there said I needed to get to Portland immediately, and I was sent by Life Flight the next day. I needed a liver transplant, and I spent the next five months there. I won't bore you with all the details, but I do feel it is necessary for you to understand the major parts of what Pam and I went through so that you know I am not writing this book as an "armchair warrior" but have been through what many of you have also experienced or will experience.

After arriving and going through more transfusions, blood tests, liver biopsies, x-rays, CT scan, MRI, and ultrasounds, my body started to swell up with fluid. My doctor came into my room, sat on my bed, and with tears in her eyes told us I had also contracted a disease called Spontaneous Bacterial Peritonitis (SBP), an acute bacterial infection you get from Ascites (fluid buildup, which had caused me to gain forty pounds). She told us to call the family because fifty percent of the people who get SBP don't ever leave the hospital. This was the first of three life threatening things I faced in that five months in Portland. I was so swollen with fluid I could not even lift my legs, they were so heavy. My bodily functions all began to shut down, and there was nothing they could do about any of it. I was taken off the transplant waiting list because the doctors thought I was not going to live. But God is not limited by the medical profession, and people were praying. The worse I became, the more they prayed. After two weeks I started to improve and finally pulled out of it. You might say, "Well, fifty percent of people DO pull out of it so how can you say God was responsible?" Because I was not heading anywhere close to a normal recovery. I was dying, and everyone knew it. There was nothing the doctors or medicine could do. God brought me through it, and it is He who gets all the glory. Amen!

During this time, my liver continued to get worse. I was so yellow from jaundice one could almost turn out the lights and see me glow! My viral count was up to sixty-nine million instead of being zero like a normal person. My liver function dropped to ten percent, and I was once again facing death. But during this period I had the greatest spiritual experience of my life, and I would like to tell you about it for the purpose of bringing hope to those who may think they have none. Remember: It is always darkest before dawn.

It was the end of the day; the shift change had taken place, and my doctors and day nurses were all going home. I could tell from their actions that many of them did not expect to see me again. Indeed, I did not expect to see them either. I did not let the extent of my feelings be known to Pam, but she was not worried anyway. She went back to the lodge where she was staying and had a good night's sleep. The Lord had given her comfort and peace before He had given it to me! That night I sat in a chair in my room unable to sleep, but I left the light off. There was just enough light coming through the windows from the lights of Portland that I could see the clock on my wall. I just sat there watching the clock and waiting for the Death Angel to strike, and the Lord to take me home. But sometime during the night I received the distinct impression that the Lord had come into my room and was standing over in a corner watching me. There was no sound, no lights flashing, no tongue talking or any other Charismatic nonsense, but there was a profound feeling of His presence. I wasn't really comforted in any special way, I just waited for the inevitable and He just watched. Much to my surprise, morning came and I was alive! The Lord's presence left, and now, after months of thinking about it, I think He came that night to do two things: (1) to keep the Death Angel from taking me, and (2) to let me know that no matter what happened, He was always with me and loves me. As a Christian I have always believed what the Lord said in the scripture - that He would never leave nor forsake me (Hebrews 13:5), but here I came face to face with that truth. What a great blessing the realization was, and it is one I will never forget.

I found out later that at the same time this was taking place, my home church, Treasure Valley Baptist, was holding special meetings with an evangelist. During his preaching that same night that I was waiting to die, the Lord spoke to Pastor DeMichele's heart and told him that I was not going to make it through the night if the church did not pray for me *that night*. So after the preaching, he announced a prayer meeting for me and several hundred people stayed to pray. The Lord gave the same message to some other friends of mine, including an inmate I had dealt with in my prison ministry. He got fifty men together (a violation of prison rules) and they also had a prayer meeting for me. I know I am alive today because of their prayers and God's love and mercy!

Jer 32:27 "Behold, I am the LORD, the God of all flesh: is there any thing too hard for me?"

The obvious answer is, no! There is nothing too hard for the Lord. Life and death are in His hands alone. A great preacher once said, "I am immortal until God is finished with me." I believe that statement with all my heart. Even death and the Devil are subject to God's will, and nothing can overcome me except my own stubborn will.

Almost a week passed. I was tired of waiting for something to happen, and my health was fading fast. Another sleepless night came and I sat in my chair once again praying. I told the Lord that whatever His will was for me, whether to live or die, it was fine with me; but could we do it NOW? I was so tired and worn out I just wanted it over one way or another. I had barely finished my prayer when my room door opened and two of my nurses entered. I had witnessed to all my nurses at some point and also to many of my doctors, and I had a great rapport with them. One nurse was jumping up and down a little and said, "They have a liver for you, and we're going to get you ready for surgery." We were all overjoyed!

But the surgery was put off and didn't take place until midnight that night and nobody seemed to know what was going on. Indeed, one of my doctors came in to talk to me, and she didn't know anything about a liver for me or surgery being scheduled. It was all a mystery, but in the mean time, I had another opportunity to witness to one of my nurses who was interested in the gospel. I found out after my surgery that she had asked the Lord to save her soul and had received Him as her personal Savior! So the delay was well worth it. Does God know what He's doing? I think He does!

The day after my surgery, I had to be opened up again to remove a large blood clot, so I ended up having major surgery two days in a row. After that, I began immediately to improve. My viral load began to drop and my liver enzymes began coming down. After four months, and many other ups and downs, infections, surgery for other problems that developed, I was released to go home. What a day of rejoicing that was. Most Christians talk about having two lives: the old one before salvation, and the new life after salvation . I have had three: those two, plus a life miraculously redeemed from death on several occasions. I had gone to the emergency room in Boise for a couple of hours to get some antibiotics; I came home five months later with someone else's liver, and medication that added up to twenty-seven pills and four insulin shots per day, plus Interferon and two other shots per week. I had developed type 2 diabetes from some of the medication I had already been on. The Interferon (a type of chemo therapy) continued for the next seven months, and my health gradually improved.

Right at the end of that seven months, my viral load was down from 69 million to 133,000. In another two weeks it should have gone to zero and the virus would be gone. What hope and rejoicing we all had. But that was not to be the end of the journey for Pam and me. In two weeks, when the lab results came back, my viral load had jumped to over two million. From there it kept going up. The Hepatitis virus had mutated and had beaten the treatment. We were all devastated! After all the miracles, prayers, rejoicing, and hope, it all went down the drain. I was once again heading for liver failure since there was no other treatment to be tried. The doctors had told me at the beginning that there was a possibility of this happening, but that the chances were remote. They said that if it did come back, it would be much more aggressive than the first time. That is what happened, and my viral load began jumping by leaps. I started making funeral arrangements.

But God was not finished showing His power, and was not done with me yet. Instead of continuing to go up, my numbers started fluctuating up and down, and they continue to do so up to the time of this writing. Some weeks they are going up and some weeks they are coming down. At times, some of them are actually in the "normal" range, and the doctors are all scratching their heads. They have no idea what is going on; but those of us who are Christians know perfectly well. God is sovereign, and will not be put into anyone's box of what should or shouldn't be.

I finally became desperate to know something from God and had a "knock down drag out" with Him in prayer for two days. I didn't care which way He wanted things to go, but I needed to know whether I needed to make living or dying plans. I put out a fleece (I know, New Testament Christians aren't supposed to do that, but I did). I laid down some very specific parameters for the fleece, and God answered it one hundred percent to the letter. He let me know that I wasn't going to die anytime soon, and I felt he was going to allow me to live out my threescore and ten years. Furthermore, I was probably going to be in this present condition that whole time.

Why doesn't He just heal me completely? That is a question that no one can answer and shouldn't even try to answer. God does nothing arbitrarily; He always has a purpose for everything He does. I do know this, my continued roller coaster ride has kept a lot of people praying, allowed me to minister to other chronically ill people, and God's grace manifest in Pam and me has been a great encouragement and inspiration to many people. How do I know that? Because hundreds of people have told us so. I know also that God has used me more since I've been sick than He was ever able to while I was healthy.

All through this trial Pam and I have prayed one thing consistently: that God would use this for His glory in some way. That is exactly what He is doing, and I wouldn't have it any other way. Would I like to be done

13

with this whole thing? Of course, who wouldn't. But I can honestly say, and have told the Lord, that I would rather stay this way and have Him continue to use me, than to have my complete health back and not be as useful to Him, 2 Corinthians 12:7-10. My testimony to all of you reading this is: trust God all the way. He loves you far beyond your ability to comprehend, and will be with you in every situation bringing grace, comfort, and possibly healing.

Addenda: a couple of months after writing the above, Dr. Sasaki, from Portland, contacted me and told me about a new drug that was in the stage before clinical trial, but one with which they were having good success. It is called Boceprevir, and is added to the regular Interferon treatment that I took last time. It is now July 2012, and I am once again in Portland for two to four months while I get started on this new treatment. So, here we go again. I must endure another seven months of Interferon treatment plus a new drug added. I am certainly not looking forward to this since the treatment last time made me so sick; and I certainly do not want to go through it again only for it to fail. But it is worth the try, therefore, by the grace of God, we go into the dark again, with only the light of the Lord Jesus Christ, and the blessings I listed above still with us.

De 33:27 "The eternal God is thy refuge, and underneath are the everlasting arms...

Chapter Two: I'm Still Trusting My Lord

> Pro 3.5-6 "Trust in the LORD with all thine heart; and lean not unto thine own understanding. In all thy ways acknowledge him, and he shall direct thy paths."

In quoting the above verse, I realize that there are many of you who suffer from chronic illness that may be tired of hearing it. How do I know that? Because there are times when I am also tired of hearing it quoted to me by well-meaning brethren. Not long ago, I was talking with one of the assistant pastors at church and he told me that he had just been talking to a church member who said, "I don't know what to say to Brother Bob." I also know that feeling, having been in the same situation many times before I was sick. People, who have never been through something like this, have no idea how to relate to those who have; and it can be an awkward time of silence, or of not knowing what to say. They pick a verse or two that they are familiar with, like this one or Romans 8:28, and quote them to us hoping that it will be a help and encouragement. And no one can fault them for it, they mean well, but just don't understand. There was a time when I was so sick of hearing Romans 8:28 that I could almost have wished it was not in the Bible. Do I believe the verse? Of course I do; I know it to be true first hand. However, well-meaning people just don't know what to say, and we have to learn to smile and say,

"Thank you, and God bless you for your prayers and concern." And mean it!

Nevertheless, the verses are true, and there are going to be times on our journey that we ARE going to have to just trust in the Lord, because we are not going to understand what is going on or why. A child like trust is all we are going to have to sustain us.

The Lord tells us in Matthew to be converted and become as little children. When a child is told to get in the car, he may ask where he is going, but he doesn't ask all the details as to how to get there; he or she simply trusts the driver to get him there. And that is exactly what the Lord wants us to do. Even though it is my nature, as a man, to want to know all the details of something, the Lord may not want me to know it all. I just have to trust the fact that HE KNOWS.

Php 4:6 "Be careful for nothing but in every thing by prayer and supplication with thanksgiving let your requests be made known unto God."

The word "careful" is used a little differently here than it is used in our time; the word simply means "don't be full of care." The Lord used my dog (yes, He did) to give me an illustration of this just this morning. While staying in the R.V., we have had a few neighbors from time to time, and we have one right now. This morning my new neighbor came out of his R.V. and my dog started barking as if there was some danger we needed to know about. I kept telling him to be quiet, but he wouldn't listen. Finally, I told him, "don't worry, "I

16

know all about it. Immediately, the Lord hit me in the head and said, "yes, stop worrying, I know all about it." I really hate it when I'm sometimes so stupid that the Lord is able to use my dog to remind or teach me something.

Brethren, we can either trust, or do the one thing that never helps in any situation – worry. And as we should all know, worry will only make a person sicker, and will upset those who are around us. Worry is the opposite of trust, and it shows a lack of confidence in the Lord. It is a sin. Sarcasm says, "Why trust when we can worry?" Brethren, it brings glory to God when He hides something from us, but we completely trust Him anyway.

Many years ago, while I was in the United States Army, I was given the opportunity to go rappelling from a helicopter with the Army Pathfinders. It promised to be quite an experience: hanging from a rope, eighty feet off the ground, attached by only a rope to the helicopter. But strangely, I had no fear about it, and enjoyed the experience immensely. Why was I without fear? Because I trusted my Pathfinder teacher to keep me safe.

> Pr 25:2 *"It is the glory of God to conceal a thing: but the honour of kings is to search out a matter."*

Search for an answer - yes. Worry about it - no. If the Lord gives you an answer to the question, great! But if He doesn't, we just have to trust that He has a good reason for not doing so.

Here is an example of having to trust God, when all the circumstances tell you that you can't.

Ex 5:22-23 "And Moses returned unto the LORD, and said, Lord, wherefore hast thou so evil entreated this people? why is it that thou hast sent me? For since I came to Pharaoh to speak in thy name, he hath done evil to this people; neither hast thou delivered thy people at all."

Moses was complaining that God didn't keep His promise to him and the people, but that God actually made things worse. And He had! Then God told him it was just going to result in a greater victory when He showed His power on Pharaoh in Exodus 6. Yes, it would be tough for awhile. But in the end, the deliverance was going to be great, and God's glory would be magnified. And so also was Moses in the sight of God, Pharaoh, and the Jewish people.

Listen to the turmoil and final victory in the following verses of King David:

Ps 42 "As the hart panteth after the water brooks, so panteth my soul after thee, O God. My soul thirsteth for God, for the living God: when shall I come and appear before God? My tears have been my meat day and night, while they continually say unto me, Where is thy God? When I remember these things, I pour out my soul in me: for I had gone with the multitude, I went with them to the house of God, with the voice of joy and praise, with a multitude that kept holyday. Why art thou cast down, O my soul? and why art thou disquieted in me? hope thou in God: for I shall yet

18

praise him for the help of his countenance. O my God, my soul is cast down within me: therefore will I remember thee from the land of Jordan, and of the Hermonites, from the hill Mizar. Deep calleth unto deep at the noise of thy waterspouts: all thy waves and thy billows are gone over me. Yet the LORD will command his lovingkindness in the daytime, and in the night his song shall be with me, and my prayer unto the God of my life. I will say unto God my rock, Why hast thou forgotten me? why go I mourning because of the oppression of the enemy? As with a sword in my bones, mine enemies reproach me; while they say daily unto me, Where is thy God? Why art thou cast down, O my soul? and why art thou disquieted within me? hope thou in God: for I shall yet praise him, who is the health of my countenance, and my God."

Sometimes we forget the whole purpose of God creating us, and we start to think the life we live is our own to do with as we choose. However, we are not our own. We are "bought with a price," and are "crucified with Christ." We were made for one purpose only: to please the One who created us (Revelation 4:11). What He chooses to do with the life He gave us is not any of our business; we are expected to turn our life over to Him to do with whatever *He* wills. Things like this:

Heb 12:5-13 "And ye have forgotten the exhortation which speaketh unto you as unto children, My son, despise not thou the chastening of the Lord, nor faint when thou art rebuked of him: For whom the Lord loveth he chasteneth, and scourgeth every son whom he receiveth. If ye endure chastening, God dealeth with you as with sons; for what son is he whom the father chasteneth not? But if ye be without chastisement, whereof all are partakers, then are ye bastards, and not sons. Furthermore we have had fathers of our flesh which corrected us, and we gave them reverence: shall we not much rather be in subjection unto the Father of spirits, and live? For they verily for a few days chastened us after their own pleasure; but he for our profit, that we might be partakers of his holiness. Now no chastening for the present seemeth to be joyous, but grievous: nevertheless afterward it yieldeth the peaceable fruit of righteousness unto them which are exercised thereby. Wherefore lift up the hands which hang down, and the feeble knees; And make straight paths for your feet, lest that which is lame be turned out of the way; but let it rather be healed."

Yes, there are going to be times when we will not like or understand God's will. There will be times when we feel, like Jesus did on the cross, that God has forsaken us. There will be times when our trust in Him will be tested to the breaking point, and possibly kept at that point for a long time. *What better proof of our love and trust?*

When I was in the aviation industry, we had a program called NDT (Non Destructive Testing). A part for an airplane would be broken to see where the point of stress fracture was. From then on, all subsequent tests would be taken to that point but not be crossed. That way, it was known if the part was defective or not without destroying it. And what does God tell us?:

> 1Co 10:13 *"There hath no temptation taken you but such as is common to man: but God is faithful, who will not suffer you to be tempted above that ye are able; but will with the temptation also make a way to escape, that ye may be able to bear it."*

At some time in our lives we will all be tested to the breaking point, but never beyond it. God will always make a way to escape before we reach that final point.

Job said, "Though He slay me, yet will I trust Him." Was God going to slay him? Not at all; in fact, He told the Devil NOT to slay him. However, Job thought there was a real possibility of it. His trust in the Lord was his escape.

Isa 43:2 "When thou passest through the waters, I will be with thee; and through the rivers, they shall not overflow thee: when thou walkest through the fire, thou shalt not be burned; neither shall the flame kindle upon thee."

21

Look at the following example of tremendous faith, love, and trust:

> Ge 22:9-12 *"And they came to the place which God had told him of; and Abraham built an altar there, and laid the wood in order, and bound Isaac his son, and laid him on the altar upon the wood. And Abraham stretched forth his hand, and took the knife to slay his son. And the angel of the LORD called unto him out of heaven, and said, Abraham, Abraham: and he said, Here am I. And he said, Lay not thine hand upon the lad, neither do thou any thing unto him: for now I know that thou fearest God, seeing thou hast not withheld thy son, thine only son from me."*

God told Abraham to offer the son that God had promised him on the altar of sacrifice! What a thing to tell someone to do. And it was going to be a three day journey to get to the place. When they arrived, and Isaac found out that *he* was the sacrifice, could he have been thinking "Though he slay me, yet will I trust him?" He was obviously allowing Abraham to do this since he was a young man and Abraham an old one. He could have easily run or fought Abraham and won. Isaac and Abraham are both examples of love, faith, and trust. They traveled three days and still deliverance didn't come. Hope must have been fading in Abraham's heart. How sick he must have felt as he grabbed that knife to kill his only son. God's promise to him was about to die

22

on the altar of his love for God. *And deliverance didn't come until the last moment, when the knife was on its way down.*

The day before this, Abraham had told his servant to wait for him, and that he *and* Isaac would be back. Abraham *knew* that even if the Lord didn't stop the sacrifice, there would be a resurrection, and Isaac trusted his father enough to allow this event to take place. Brethren, even if the Lord doesn't stop us from dying on the altar of our love for Him, rest assured, there is a resurrection coming for us! Look at the story of Lazarus in John 11.

Jn 11:4 "When Jesus heard that, he said, This sickness is not unto death, but for the glory of God, that the Son of God might be glorified thereby."

Jn 11:14 "Then said Jesus unto them plainly, Lazarus is dead."

Lazarus did die; but that was not the end of the story. There was a resurrection! There was great victory in *apparent* tragedy. The same would have been true for the disciples on the Sea of Galilee. They were worried they were going to die; but, even if they had, there would have been a resurrection. The Lord told them before they entered the boat that they were going over to the other side. That's why He rebuked them for their lack of faith. They were worried they were going to die, and the circumstances absolutely showed them to be right. But they forgot the Lord's words and became fearful. If they had realized that He was the author of the storm, they would have known they weren't going to perish and could have relaxed and enjoyed the storm in a way they never had before.

In the case of Lazarus, how confused the disciples must have been for the Lord to say the sickness of Lazarus was not unto death, and then two days later He told them that Lazarus was dead! There was no way for them to understand what was going on, and the Lord offered no explanation. What else could they do but trust Him, or argue with Him that He had lied to them? As I said at the beginning of this chapter, sometimes the Lord's will is going to be way beyond our ability to understand it. *"Trust in the Lord with all thine heart..."* may be the only thing you have to hold onto sometimes.

Isa 55:9 "For as the heavens are higher than the earth, so are my ways higher than your ways, and my thoughts than your thoughts."

Brethren, make this your motto in life: No Surrender! Make it the theme of your life, as I have made it mine. **Never surrender your trust in the Lord to your thoughts and emotions.** Never surrender your trust in the promises of God to the Devil and his lies. Never surrender your trust to brethren that are not as spiritual as they think they are, and that say your affliction is caused by some hidden sin. Job's friends did that to him and almost drove the man mad. And in the end, God rebuked them for accusing Job falsely. Perhaps your affliction *is caused* by some sin in your life, but that is for you and God to determine and sort out. But even if it is,

Christ still loves you; and there is always abundant forgiveness for true repentance. He loves you, and the more you trust Him, the closer it will bring you to Him.

I was recently talking to a dear brother in the Lord who had been afflicted and had to give up his ministry. After twenty-five years of full-time ministry, he was now barely scraping by financially with his wife working a minimum wage job. He had lost his ability to do almost everything, including driving a car. He was pretty upset the day I talked with him because the Devil was trying to convince him that his affliction was due to some sin in his life. He started telling me about some of the minor things in his life for which he thought God was punishing him. However, the things he mentioned were things that every person on this planet suffers from; I told him if God was punishing him for those things then we were all being punished! I told him that if that was all there was, God wasn't punishing him, the Devil was just trying to make him *think* God was. If there was really some sin that God was punishing him for, God would be pretty cruel to not give him the reason for doing so. No good father would do that to his child.

However, it is difficult at times to believe that you are still right with God, and right where you're supposed to be, when your whole life is falling apart around you. Brethren, if you find no concrete reason for God to be punishing you, then don't cast away your confidence and trust in God. Don't surrender to the lies of the Devil. Continue trusting God! Take the lemons you've been given and make lemonade out of them. **God deserves the victory of His Saints to throw back in the face of the Devil!** Will you give Him that victory?

Chapter Three:
Discouragement

> Ps 13:1-6 How long wilt thou forget me, O LORD? for ever? how long wilt thou hide thy face from me? How long shall I take counsel in my soul, *having* sorrow in my heart daily? how long shall mine enemy be exalted over me? Consider *and* hear me, O LORD my God: lighten mine eyes, lest I sleep the sleep of death; Lest mine enemy say, I have prevailed against him; *and* those that trouble me rejoice when I am moved. But I have trusted in thy mercy; my heart shall rejoice in thy salvation. I will sing unto the LORD, because he hath dealt bountifully with me."

Have you ever noticed how many of David's Psalms start off with a discouraged heart, and end up with a rejoicing one? It is almost universal in David's Psalms. The circumstances showed there was no hope, but in the God of circumstances there is always hope.

I've read that the Japanese have an unequivocal way of looking at discouragement. They say "Discouragement is defeat of the mind." What a true statement that is! Discouragement is nothing more than our minds telling us things like: there's no hope, God doesn't understand or care, my life is over, I'm just a burden to people now, the promises of Scripture are a lie, I'm better off dead than alive, I should just give up and die, and many more. How do I know that? I know that because all of those thoughts have been my own at one point or another during my journey. You may ask me, "Even as a minister you doubted the Bible to be true at times? You wanted to just give up and die? You thought God was through with you and your life was over?" Yes, I had all those thoughts and many more, including thoughts of suicide.

Am I alone in those feelings? Am I backslidden? Am I a terrible Christian because I think such things?
Listen to the words of one of the greatest preachers and ministers the world has ever known:

"Fits of depression come over the most of *us.* Cheerful as we may be, we must at intervals be cast down. The strong are not always vigorous, the wise not always ready, the brave not always courageous, and the joyous not always happy.

"There may be here and there men of iron to whom wear and tear work no perceptible detriment, but surely the rust frets even these; and as for ordinary men, the Lord knows and makes them to know that they are but dust.

"Knowing by most painful experience what deep depression of spirit means, being visited therewith at seasons by no means few or far between, I thought it might be consolatory to some of my brethren if I gave my thoughts thereon, that younger men might not fancy that some strange thing had happened to them when they became for a season possessed by melancholy; and that sadder men might know that one

upon whom the sun has shone right joyously did not always walk in the light.

"It is not necessary by quotations from the biographies of eminent ministers to prove that seasons of fearful prostration have fallen to the lot of most, if not all, of them.

"The life of Luther might suffice to give a thousand instances, and he was by no means of the weaker sort. His great spirit was often in the seventh heaven of exultation, and as frequently on the borders of despair. His very deathbed was not free from tempests, and he sobbed himself into his last sleep like a greatly wearied child."

Taken from: When a Preacher is Downcast
by Charles H. Spurgeon
[italics mine]

Much of our "Fight For Life" will be won or lost in our hearts and minds.

Listen to the words of the greatest king Israel ever had, King David:

Ps 55.4-7 "My heart is sore pained within me: and the terrors of death are fallen upon me. Fearfulness and trembling are come upon me, and horror hath overwhelmed me. And I said, Oh that I had wings like a dove! for then would I fly away, and be at rest. Lo, then would I wander far off, and remain in the wilderness. Selah."

29

Ps 40:12 "For innumerable evils have compassed me about: mine iniquities have taken hold upon me, so that I am not able to look up; they are more than the hairs of mine head: therefore my heart faileth me."

And of one of the greatest Christians that has ever lived, the Apostle Paul:

2Co 1:8-9 "For we would not, brethren, have you ignorant of our trouble which came to us in Asia, that we were pressed out of measure, above strength, insomuch that we despaired even of life: But we had the sentence of death in ourselves, that we should not trust in ourselves, but in God which raiseth the dead:"

2Co 4:8-10 "We are troubled on every side, yet not distressed; we are perplexed, but not in despair; Persecuted, but not forsaken; cast down, but not destroyed; Always bearing about in the body the dying of the Lord Jesus, that the life also of Jesus might be made manifest in our body."

Discouragement is no respecter of persons. There are a few, as Spurgeon said, that do not seem to succumb to it, however, "the exception always proves the rule."

In the Old Testament, Joseph in prison should serve as an example to us all, but his spirit is not an easy one to emulate. Lied about, forgotten by those whom he helped, sold by his brothers; he never gave up or went into despair. He had an indomitable spirit, and is one of, if not the only example in the Bible (besides that of the Lord Jesus Christ), who did not become discouraged at his circumstances.

Perhaps we can look into his heart and see a vision of the future given by God and a passage of scripture about his journey.

Ps 105:17-22 "He sent a man before them, even Joseph, who was sold for a servant: Whose feet they hurt with fetters: he was laid in iron: Until the time that his word came: <u>the word of the LORD tried him.</u> The king sent and loosed him; even the ruler of the people, and let him go free. He made him lord of his house, and ruler of all his substance: To bind his princes at his pleasure; and teach his senators wisdom."

The *"word of the Lord tried him"*? It seems Joseph knew he was being tested and prepared by God for some greater purpose. The Lord had given him dreams and visions of greatness when he was a young man. He had a message from God that he would one day be a leader of his brethren, and he never seems to have doubted that message.

Have the promises of God seemed a lie to you at times? Are the Devil and your flesh doing all they can to get you to "curse God and die"? Are there times when you just want to say "I don't care what God wants, I've had enough"? Do not despair, dear friend, only the exceptions to the rule have never done so, and those exceptions are very few and far between. You are not a reprobate, backslidder, or a terrible Christian for thinking those things. You are a human being. God understands you perfectly, a*nd He is not angry with you because of it.* He was not angry with any of the men in the examples He gave us, and He's not angry with you either. Don't let the Devil talk you into believing that lie. God loved you before you knew Him, in spite of what you were; and He doesn't love you any less now, even when we don't always do the things that please Him.

1Pe 5:7 "Casting all your care upon him; for he careth for you."

Discouragement is a "care" like any other, and you can give it to Him, being assured that He will not refuse to help you with it.

Pr 23:26 "My son, give me thine heart, and let thine eyes observe my ways."

Pr 4:23 "Keep thy heart with all diligence; for out of it are the issues of life."

Always try to keep in mind our perfect example, the Lord Jesus Christ. When He faced His greatest trial, one that caused Him to sweat great drops of blood, He knew His Father was the Author and Finisher of the trial, and He did not just accept, but embraced the will of the Father.

Jn 12:27 "Now is my soul troubled; and what shall I say? Father, save me from this hour: but for this cause came I unto this hour."

"Keep thy heart with all diligence." This is not some accident that has happened to you without God's knowledge or permission. Don't let circumstances dictate your faith. Christ was troubled about his circumstances, yes; and we cannot expect to have fewer trials happen to us. But we do not have to let these feelings consume and control us.

1Co 10:13 "There hath no temptation taken you but such as is common to man: but God is faithful, who will not suffer you to be tempted above that ye are able; but will with the temptation also make a way to escape, that ye may be able to bear it."

I do not agree with the standard teaching of this verse which says you will never experience something more than you can handle. My experience shows that to be untrue. I rather believe it is saying that there *will* be temptations you cannot handle, but nothing that you cannot handle by the escape provided in the Lord Jesus Christ. But it is up to you whether or not you chose to use that escape. There may be, at times, a physical way to escape provided by the Lord, such as in the case of temptation by a man or woman. In that situation all you have to do to escape is do as Joseph did, RUN! All you have to do to stop drinking or smoking is just STOP. I know, it's not that easy because you're addicted, right?

After fifteen years of smoking, I was also addicted, and God told me to stop. I threw the cigarettes, beer, and drugs out the car window and just stopped. *Through Him*, you can also have victory, unless the verse is a lie, or you have a very severe addiction that could cause damage to you by going cold turkey. In that case a physician could be the *way to escape* that God has prepared. Prayer and good counsel will have to be your guides in that case.

During my journey to try to get well I became addicted to pain killers and sleeping pills, neither of which I really needed anymore. When I realized it, I informed my doctor that I was going to quit using them. She told me I would probably need help because going "cold turkey" would be very difficult. However, in that difficulty I saw yet another opportunity to show the power of God in my life, so I went the cold turkey route. Was it a hard road? Not really; I didn't sleep for several nights, and was pretty uncomfortable being used to the numbness of the pain killers, but God's grace is always sufficient, and He helped me through. Now before I go any further, please note that I said I did not really need those things any longer. I am not advocating getting off of any medication that you NEED. The Apostle Paul carried a physician (Luke) with him all the time, and I'm sure Paul did as Luke prescribed. If a physician tells you that you need something, then you should heed his advice. However, in my case, they were no longer needed.

God has promised you an escape from every temptation, and *"casting all your care upon Him"* IS the escape. Prayer IS the escape. Determination not to sin against God IS the escape. Faith IS the escape.

Discouragement is not a physical malady in itself, it is a mental one. Your escape is not found in taking anti-depressants (as they put me on for awhile, and which I finally threw away), it is in Jesus Christ. Prayer, good counsel, and the encouragement of good friends and family can be a help at times, but even these will break down eventually. Only God can get you through some things on your journey, and you must learn to "cast your care upon him" and *leave it there!*

> Deut 33.27 *"The eternal God is thy refuge, and underneath are the everlasting arms: and he shall thrust out the enemy from before thee; and shall say, Destroy them."*

Allow me to give you one more example.

Darlene Diebler Rose was a missionary to Indonesia when WWII broke out. She and other missionaries refused to leave their station, and were eventually taken prisoner by the Japanese Army. There are many things that happen to a missionary, especially a female, that she would not mention; but the things she did talk about were horrific circumstances for anyone to have to go through: starvation, beatings, her husband dying, fire and shrapnel bombings by American forces, women losing their minds, no medical supplies, etc. She triumphed over that terrible ordeal in one way. I will let her words describe it:

> There were many times when I thought, during those years, that God had left me, that God had forsaken me. But the moment that I took my eyes off of the circumstances that surrounded me, and I looked up, there He stood, on the parapet of Heaven. Never for a moment was I out of His sight.
>
> Darlene Rose
> Radio Broadcast

Therein lies the secret to beating the problem of discouragement, taking our eyes off the circumstances in which we find ourselves, and looking up to the Lord.

Heb 12:11-13 "Now no chastening for the present seemeth to be joyous, but grievous: nevertheless afterward it yieldeth the peaceable fruit of righteousness unto them which are exercised thereby. Wherefore lift up the hands which hang down, and the feeble knees; And make straight paths for your feet, lest that which is lame be turned out of the way; but let it rather be healed."

Ps 121:1-2 "I will lift up mine eyes unto the hills, from whence cometh my help. My help cometh from the LORD, which made heaven and earth."

Chapter Four: Think On These Things

So, how do we keep our thoughts on the right path? How do we avoid discouragement? One thing that is a great help is keeping the right attitude and not dwelling on negative things. In some Christian circles the power of positive thinking is spoken of with distain as if it were an evil plague to be avoided at all costs. At the same time, the power of negative thinking is lifted up as the path our minds should follow in order to have the proper outlook on life. Since that was my normal, human way of looking at things anyway, that philosophy took deep root in my psyche, and I looked at everything in life from a negative standpoint. As a result, I was always in a bad mood, always complaining that something wasn't right, always criticizing just about everything (including myself), and was living a generally unhappy life. The Bible was also held up to me as a negative book! Granted, the Bible does have very little good to say about the nature of man, the way of life, and the way it ends up for lost people. It *is* a book of death and judgment. However, it is *also* a book of life, peace, joy, and a marvelous future for the saved. I don't find one passage of scripture in the entire Bible commanding, or even recommending us to think on negative things. On the contrary we find this:

Php 4:6-9 "Be careful for nothing; but in every thing by prayer and supplication with thanksgiving let your requests be made known unto God. And the peace of God, which passeth all understanding, shall keep your hearts and minds through Christ Jesus. Finally, brethren, whatsoever things are true, whatsoever things *are* honest, whatsoever things *are* just, whatsoever things *are* pure, whatsoever things *are* lovely, whatsoever things *are* of good report; if *there be* any virtue, and if *there be* any praise, think on these things. Those things, which ye have both learned, and received, and heard, and seen in me, do: and the God of peace shall be with you."

Notice there isn't *one negative thing in the entire list!* The scripture says: "Looking unto Jesus; I will lift UP mine eyes; Come unto me all ye that labour...I'll give you REST; Thou wilt keep *him* in PERFECT PEACE, *whose* mind *is* stayed *on thee*: because he trusteth in thee;" and many more verses of a *positive* nature. If you want real healing and peace in your spirit, a negative outlook is not going to produce it.

Pr 18:14 "The spirit of a man will sustain his infirmity; but a wounded spirit who can bear?"

Pr 15:13 A merry heart maketh a cheerful countenance: but by sorrow of the heart the spirit is broken.

Pr 15:15 All the days of the afflicted are evil: but he that is of a merry heart hath a continual feast.

Right from the beginning of the Book we find both the negative and positive side of things, and we need to be aware of both sides and how to use them in our attitude. Adam and Eve are the first examples we have of human experience and we see both sides of the equation in their lives.

The negative side is that they disobeyed God, damned the entire human race, and brought death into the world with the killing of an animal for its skin to cover their shame. If you are a student of the Bible then you see an implication that the animal was a lamb that was used to cover the result of their sin.

And in that we also see the positive side: God forgives sinners and makes a way for restoring fellowship and eternal life. *"Behold the Lamb of God that taketh away the sin of the world!"* It may have been a negative action on Adam and Eve's part, but the mercy and love of God (which should be our focus) results in a positive ending.

The story of Noah and the Ark is the same. Yes, the world became so evil that the Lord found it necessary to destroy the entire population. But again, we see the mercy of God and a picture of salvation in the ark. The Lord Jesus Christ is our ark, and through Him we can escape the judgment of God that is coming on all the world.

Abraham and Isaac also serve as an example. What a negative thing it would be to have God tell you to kill your own child. But in it we see the trust of both

Abraham and Isaac; Abraham's trust in God and Isaac's trust in his father. And the result is that once again we have a picture of salvation and God's mercy.

When Isaac asked where the lamb for the sacrifice was, Abraham responded with, "*God will provide Himself a Lamb.*" Isaac must have willingly allowed Abraham to bind him since Abraham was an old man and Isaac a young one, just as Jesus Christ willingly went to the cross to obey His Father.

As the knife of Abraham's obedience was on its way down, God stopped him, and in essence said, "*Abraham, you don't have to kill your son, I'll kill mine instead.*" Then a ram miraculously appeared and took Isaac's place on the altar. A ram is the father of a lamb!

The Bible a negative book? Certainly, but the positive side far outweighs the negative, and that is where we are told to focus our attention. Doesn't the scripture itself tell us, "*...I would have you wise unto that which is good, and simple concerning evil*" – Romans 16:19.

How can we say "The joy of the Lord" is our strength when there is little joy in our hearts because we are focused on the negative side of life? Aren't we to show the victory we have in Christ to those around us as a testimony to the grace of God in our lives? The scripture says "*Let the redeemed of the Lord say so.*" Now, this is NOT an endorsement of some liberal's positive thinking books. Many times they will take the positive promises that God makes to His children and apply them to lost people. By doing that, they are helping to seal a person's fate by making them think they are justified in God's sight; when, in reality, they are under His condemnation. No, I am not advocating that position at all. Rather, this is an endorsement of the power of "thinking positively" about the promises that God has given to those of us who are saved, and toward God Himself. The scripture also says this: Pr 4:23 *"Keep thy heart with all diligence; for out of it are the issues of life."* What is in your heart will show in your life. If there is joy in your heart it will show in the way you live.

Look at the following passage of scripture and you will see both sides of the equation. In the first ten verses the psalmist is making his complaint about all his troubles. And I know that some of you reading this can well relate to what he says, having had, or having now, many of the same feelings of despair, discouragement, and hopelessness.

Ps 77 "I cried unto God with my voice, even unto God with my voice; and he gave ear unto me. In the day of my trouble I sought the Lord: my sore ran in the night, and ceased not: my soul refused to be comforted. I remembered God, and was troubled: I complained, and my spirit was overwhelmed. Selah. Thou holdest mine eyes waking: I am so troubled that I cannot speak. I have considered the days of old, the years of ancient times. I call to remembrance my song in the night: I commune with mine own heart: and my spirit made diligent search. Will the Lord cast off for ever? and will he be favourable no more? Is his mercy clean gone for ever? doth his promise fail for evermore? Hath God forgotten to be gracious? hath he in anger shut up his tender mercies? Selah.

But notice the victory of the same man in the next ten verses of the same Psalm when he takes his mind off himself and starts thinking about the Lord.

"And I said, This is my infirmity: *but I will remember* the years of the right hand of the most High. I will remember the works of the LORD: surely I will remember thy wonders of old. I will meditate also of all thy work, and talk of thy doings. Thy way, O God, is in the sanctuary: who is so great a God as *our* God? Thou *art* the God that doest wonders: thou hast declared thy strength among the people. Thou hast with *thine* arm redeemed thy people, the sons of Jacob and Joseph. Selah. The waters saw thee, O God, the waters saw thee; they were afraid: the depths also were troubled. The clouds poured out water: the skies sent out a sound: thine arrows also went abroad. The voice of thy thunder *was* in the heaven: the lightnings lightened the world: the earth trembled and shook. Thy way *is* in the sea, and thy path in the great waters, and thy footsteps are not known. Thou leddest thy people like a flock by the hand of Moses and Aaron."

The peace and victory to overcome our problems comes from focusing our attention on the positive side of things, not the negative.

Ps 55:22 "Cast thy burden upon the LORD, and he shall sustain thee: he shall never suffer the righteous to be moved."

Keep your eyes on the Lord! Amen?   Something that helps me do that is to go out into the natural world and find illustrations of God in everything He made.

Ps 19:1 The heavens declare the glory of God; and the firmament sheweth his handywork."

You will never have a clear picture of yourself until you have a clearer picture of God, and the natural world is a great help in revealing God to us in ways we can understand.

Just in the last two days the Lord has given me some illustrations of Him and the Christian life through some things I observed. Let me illustrate.

Right near the R.V. in which we are staying is a war memorial garden, and I go there every day to think and pray. Yesterday, while walking through there I noticed some berry bushes. And what was on the bush besides fruit and leaves? Thorns. Lots of thorns. A simple illustration of the Christian life: you cannot pick most fruit without having to deal with thorns. You will get stuck to one extent or another. If you want fruit in your Christian life, you are going to have to deal with thorns along the way. Now, that is just a simple illustration, but what would you have seen if you had looked at the same berry bush? Would you have pondered anything about it, or just passed it by without a thought?

Another illustration is found in a simple drop of water. The pictures of the Trinity in water are abundant for anyone to see, but how many people take the time to look and think about it. Water is an essential life giving element to all human beings. You absolutely cannot live without it. The majority of our bodies, and the planet we call home, are made up of this simple element. Allow me to illustrate:

1. Nothing in this world can live without it. In John 15:5 Jesus tells us that without Him, we can do nothing.
2. Water is one substance composed of three parts: two hydrogen molecules and one oxygen. The Trinity is one Entity made up of three parts: God the Father, God the Son, and God the Holy Spirit.
3. Water is found in three major locations: oceans, lakes, and rivers.
4. It can take on three different forms: solid, liquid, and gas.
5. Water is free, it comes down from God. Revelation 22:17 says: *"And whosoever will, let him take the water of life freely."*

Some other illustrations of the Trinity are these:
1. A flower. It is made up of three basic parts: a root, a stem, and a flower.
2. The Earth is land, sea, and sky.
3. A family is a father, mother, and children.
4. The Bible tells us in 1 Thessalonians 5:23 that a person is made up of body, soul, and spirit.
5. Our bodies are flesh, bones, and blood.
6. The sun, that also gives life on earth, gives off three kinds of rays: alpha, beta, gamma. It gives light, heat, and ultra-violet rays. Jesus Christ is called the *"Sun of righteousness"* in Malachi 4:2.

When someone says to me that they cannot find God, it tells me they are not really looking for Him. God is everywhere, and He will reveal Himself to anyone who truly looks for Him.

Nothing earth shattering was revealed in those illustrations, but it was a blessing to me to sit quietly and have something as simple as a glass of water bring the Creator of the universe to my mind. And again I wonder how many people have looked at a flower and seen the greatness of God illustrated in it? Simple illustrations, but I never would have seen them if I had been focused on negative or minor things instead of looking for God.

When you can see God illustrated all around you, it certainly helps to keep your mind focused on positive things, and helps your attitude immensely.

Will I ever be completely healed of my disease and the consequences it has had on my body? No. I will always have someone else's liver inside me, I will be on anti-rejection medication for the rest of my life, and my stomach and intestinal tract will never be the same again from all the medication I've taken. Furthermore, unless some new treatment is developed, or the Lord gives me a miraculous healing, I will always have Hepatitis, and I will never have the strength and stamina I had before all these events happened. So, should I dwell on these things in my heart and walk around with a disfigured face like the Pharisees did to let everyone know they were fasting? Should I complain to everyone how bad I feel most of the time? Should I look at my own circumstances and feel sorry for myself because of them? Will thinking on these things serve to make my life better and more joyful? Will it benefit anyone around me? Negative thinking will not serve to benefit any of these situations, and will only serve to make me a grumpy old man.

What should I think of in my circumstances? Shall I give you a list?

1. I'm alive and I should be dead. I asked God to spare my life for the sake of others, and He did.
2. I asked God to use this journey for His honor and glory, and He is. Pam and I have had many, many people tell us what a blessing and encouragement we have been to them because we haven't given up, and they can see God working in our lives.
3. God has given me a new ministry to the chronically ill. I can understand what they are going through because I've walked in their shoes.
4. I have a closer, more personal relationship with the Lord Jesus Christ than I've ever had.
5. My preaching and teaching are better than they ever have been because I now have a better understanding of life, God, and people's experiences in life than I had before.
6. I appreciate life more, and am more content with where I am, what I am, what I have, and what my future is than I've ever been.
7. For someone that can hardly spell his own name, here I sit writing a book that will hopefully be a blessing and help to many others.
8. I've learned, even more than I already knew, just how great a wife Pam is to me.
9. I've learned to appreciate and love my family more than ever.
10. I know that God is in total control of my entire situation.

11. I'm saved, eternally secure, and will one day have a perfect body.
12. Jesus Christ is my savior, brother, and friend...

That's not a bad list for a start, and if I sit and think about it, I will be able to list many more reasons.
How would your list read?
Why in the world should I think on negative things that lead to discouragement and despair when I can think on all those things instead?

> Ps 5:11 *"But let all those that put their trust in thee rejoice: let them ever shout for joy, because thou defendest them: let them also that love thy name be joyful in thee."*

Oh the joy of the Power of Positive Thinking! Practice it, and make it a permanent part of your life if you want to find the peace that passes all understanding.

Chapter Five: Words of Encouragement

This chapter is written to help you accomplish the things I mentioned in the last chapter above. Remember, there is always a positive to every negative. A automobile cannot have a battery that has only a positive or negative post; it must have both. It is illustrated quite well for us in the following passage:

2Co 4:8-18 *"We are troubled on every side, yet not distressed; we are perplexed, but not in despair; Persecuted, but not forsaken; cast down, but not destroyed; Always bearing about in the body the dying of the Lord Jesus, that the life also of Jesus might be made manifest in our body. For we which live are alway delivered unto death for Jesus' sake, that the life also of Jesus might be made manifest in our mortal flesh. So then death worketh in us, but life in you. We having the same spirit of faith, according as it is written, I believed, and therefore have I spoken; we also believe, and therefore speak; Knowing that he which raised up the Lord Jesus shall raise up us also by Jesus, and shall present us with you. For all things are for your sakes, that the abundant grace might through the thanksgiving of many redound to the glory of God. For which cause we faint not; but though our outward man perish, yet the inward man is renewed day by day. For our light affliction, which is but for a moment, worketh for us a far more exceeding and eternal weight of glory; While we look not at the things which are seen, but at the things which are not seen: for the things which are seen are temporal; but the things which are not seen are eternal."*

Please look at the victory Paul has in those verses. He looks at both the negative and positive side of things, but knows that the outcome of every situation for a Christian is a positive one. He is, after all, the one who penned Romans 8:28! The eternal struggle for a Christian is always between darkness and light, good and evil, black and white, negative and positive. And Paul constantly reminds himself that even though life is pretty negative at times, still, God is in control. John tells us that *"God is light, and in Him is no darkness at all"* – 1 John 1:5.

Take courage, my dear friend! For a Christian, even in death there is a glorious resurrection! One of my favorite passages is this:

Pr 23:18 "For surely there is an end; and thine expectation shall not be cut off."

Life will not always be this way with its ups and downs. The promises of God are true, and you can rest your weary soul on them. The future is filled with nothing but positive things once we get through the veil of death.

Re 21:1-5 "*And I saw a new heaven and a new earth: for the first heaven and the first earth were passed away; and there was no more sea. And I John saw the holy city, new Jerusalem, coming down from God out of heaven, prepared as a bride adorned for her husband. And I heard a great voice out of heaven saying, Behold, the tabernacle of God is with men, and he will dwell with them, and they shall be his people, and God himself shall be with them, and be their God. And God shall wipe away all tears from their eyes; and there shall be no more death, neither sorrow, nor crying, neither shall there be any more pain: for the former things are passed away. And he that sat upon the throne said, Behold, I make all things new. And he said unto me, Write: for these words are true and faithful.*"*

In 1 Samuel 30 David and his men have been running from King Saul and are living in the land of the Philistines. While he and his men went off to war, the Amalekites invaded his home town and took all his, and his men's wives, children, and possessions away. When the men returned they were so distraught they even talked of stoning David. And what did David do? Verse six says: David encouraged himself in the LORD his God. No crying, no complaining, no threats of vengeance: just prayer and trust. In fact, David asked the Lord if he should pursue after the Amalekites or not! And the Lord told him to pursue, but what if the Lord had told him not to? If you know the character of David, and his love for God, then you would know that David would have obeyed and let them go. You may say, "What a terrible thing for him to do!" No, David just trusted God completely and knew, like Abraham did with Isaac, that God would work it all out some other way. That is trust. That is encouraging yourself in the Lord.

Here are just a few more "exceeding great and precious promises":

Hebrews 13:5 "Let your conversation be without covetousness; and be content with such things as ye have: for he hath said, 1 will never leave thee, nor forsake thee."

✞

Matthew 11:28 "Come unto me, all ye that labour and are heavy laden, and 1 will give you rest."

✞

Isaiah 26:3 "Thou wilt keep him in perfect peace, whose mind is stayed on thee: because he trusteth in thee."

✞

Jn 14:27 "Peace 1 leave with you, my peace 1 give unto you: not as the world giveth, give 1 unto you. Let not your heart be troubled, neither let it be afraid."

✞

Notice in the above verse that the Lord's peace is different from anything you will find in the world.

Php 3:20-4:1 "For our conversation is in heaven; from whence also we look for the Saviour, the Lord Jesus Christ: Who shall change our vile body, that it may be fashioned like unto his glorious body, according to the working whereby he is able even to subdue all things unto himself. Therefore, my brethren dearly beloved and longed for, my joy and crown, so stand fast in the Lord, my dearly beloved."

✝

Sometimes it seems like there is no end to the suffering, pain, and sorrow in our lives. And we must keep reminding ourselves that it is the Devil that puts those thoughts in us, and we must be constantly aware of his tactics. He wants us to focus on our present circumstances, and persuade us to stop trusting the Lord.

Heb 10:35 "Cast not away therefore your confidence, which hath great recompence of reward."

My pastor, Rick DeMichele, tells us frequently that we have two choices. We can "cast away our cares" (1 Peter 5:7), or we can "cast away our confidence."

"Care" or "confidence," which would you prefer? Because *it is up to you.* David encouraged *himself* in the Lord. Encouraging yourself is obviously something that only you can do. Others can try to help you, like Aaron and Hur holding up the hands of Moses in the battle with the Amalekites (Exodus 17), but sometimes we are so weary with it all that we don't even want to be encouraged. We just want to wallow in our own self-pity.

Brethren, that is the "slough of despond" and the Devil's playground. Only *you* can prevent becoming a resident of despair.

> 1Th 5:16-21 "Rejoice evermore. Pray without ceasing. In every thing give thanks: for this is the will of God in Christ Jesus concerning you. Quench not the Spirit. Despise not prophesyings. Prove all things; hold fast that which is good."

Chapter Six: From "Why" To "What"

> Ps 119:67 *"Before I was afflicted I went astray: but now have I kept thy word."*

Why? Ah yes, the eternal question – "why." Why me, Lord? Why now? Why did it have to be cancer? Why do I have to suffer, especially since I've tried to be a good Christian? Why does my family have to go through this? Why us when we have no medical insurance?

Would you allow me to say something you may not want to hear, and still stay with me through the rest of the chapter? The question "why" only brings discouragement, sorrow, and bitterness. It is a question that is rarely ever answered, and one with which we will drive ourselves, and those around us, out of our minds trying to figure out.

The question "why has the Lord let this happen" is a question of despair, not of hope; a question that comes from the thought of not having a future; a fear of the pain, sickness, and sorrow that is sure to come. Brethren, try to get it settled in your heart right now that the Lord will most likely not give you the answer to that question. And if He does answer it, normally it will not be for a long time down the road. However, there is one answer to that question that I would like to briefly touch on. It is found here:

1Pe 4:1-2 "Forasmuch then as Christ hath suffered for us in the flesh, arm yourselves likewise with the same mind: for he that hath suffered in the flesh hath ceased from sin; That he no longer should live the rest of his time in the flesh to the lusts of men, but to the will of God."

Many times the answer to "why" is to break our desire to live unto ourselves and turn our lives over to God's complete control. I will discuss this subject in depth in chapter 10, so I will leave it alone for the time being.

Other than that reason, why doesn't He answer what we perceive as a desperate need to know? Because knowing would not bring peace, and would most likely drive us away from the path God wants us to take.

I heard an old time preacher once say, "Young preachers come to me all the time telling me they are searching for the will of God in their lives." And what he told them usually didn't satisfy them, but it is true nonetheless. He would say, "Don't worry about it. If you knew what His will was, you'd probably run from it anyway! "Just get busy right where you are, and do what you can, and when God is ready for you He'll let you know." That is good advice for all of us because God is not going to reveal anything to us about His will until it's time for us to know anyway. And then we won't have to search for the answer; He will make it abundantly clear.

The real question we should be asking is not "why," but "what." The question "why" only brings discouragement, sorrow, and bitterness, but the question "what" brings understanding and hope.

What does God want me to learn from this? How can this make me a better, stronger, Christian? How can God use this in my life for the benefit of others and for the glory of God?

The "what" question will eventually draw us closer and make us more useful to Him than we ever have been. In my own life I never understood or felt much compassion for people who had a disability of some sort, because it is something that is impossible to understand unless you have walked that path. I simply did not know what it was like. The old saying is "you pay for what you don't know." But when I started getting sick, all of that began to change.

I remember waking one night with blood running down my nose and onto my pillow. Because of my disease my blood platelets had dropped so low my blood would not clot. I jumped up and ran to the bathroom but could not get the bleeding stopped. The doctors had told me told me there was a possibility of "bleeding out" if this kind of thing happened. So there I was, faced with the possibility of bleeding to death before I could get to the hospital. All of a sudden I started thinking about a lady in our church that was dying of cancer, and I wondered if she was awake at that hour suffering with something. I began to pray for her, and soon my own bleeding stopped and I was able to go back to bed. Would I ever have thought of that lady, or been praying for her at 2:00 AM, if I had not been awake and suffering myself? Lord, what is the purpose of my suffering? Learning to pray and have compassion on others? That's not a bad result of being sick!

Since then I've started a small ministry of visiting chronically ill people in our church (and anyone else brought to my attention). Most of the time I just sit and listen, and then try to be a blessing to them. But many times just having someone to talk to that understands what they are going through is all the help they need. I've found that chronically ill people all have a common set of things they face regardless of their type of illness. Only someone that faces those same things can really minister to them. Even their spouse cannot really understand; they have their own set of things to deal with, and those are things that I cannot fully understand. What are the inner heartaches Pam has faced as a result of all that has happened, the things she's had to do, and possibilities she may have to deal with in the future? How can I understand that? But together, we have a unique ability to minister to a group that not many other people can reach; Pam to the caregivers, and me to the sick. And it is a great privilege. We take them flowers, a book about healing by Henry Frost, a couple of sermons on CD, and a music CD that helped get me through the worst periods of my illness. To see their faces, the tears of joy just being able to talk to someone that understands, the fact that someone outside their family cares enough to visit them and bring them a small gift, and the comfort they receive is a great blessing to them and to Pam and me. "What" is the question to ask; not "why." If I had asked "why" I would still be asking the same question. But by asking "what," the Lord opened a door to a new ministry and chapter of our lives.

Another part of my ministry has been prison work. My doctor will not allow me to go into the "general population" area where I can mingle with the inmates as I used to do, but I can still go from cell to cell in the Maximum Security prison where there is a solid steel door between myself and the inmate. That way the possibility of disease transfer from them to me is remote. This ministry is doubly effective because I lived the life of an outlaw, dealing drugs for many years. That is, in fact, how I contracted Hepatitis. It is also effective because many of the inmates also have Hepatitis, or some other chronic disease, and I can relate to them on that level also. So even though I've never spent time in jail or prison, I still understand a portion of their lives that many people do not; and it gives me an opportunity to minister that most people will never have.

"Why" did God allow this to happen? That question is still unanswerable. "What" can He do with me now that this has happened? The answer is: He can use me to accomplish some things that very few people can. I have a power from God now to accomplish something that I never would have had without being sick, 2 Cor 12:7.

2Co 1:4 "Who comforteth us in all our tribulation, that we may be able to comfort them which are in any trouble, by the comfort wherewith we ourselves are comforted of God."

The classic Biblical example of asking "why" is found in the story of Job. Although Job never actually asked the question in the book, his own verbal justification of his life, and the answer God finally gave him, show that "why" was the real question of Job's heart. Job's diatribe from chapter 3-31 show his thoughts clearly. Job *was* a good man. The Lord tells us that in 1:1 and 1:8. His problem was *he knew he was a good man and was proud of it.* His following argument with God is typical: "Lord, I'm a good man, and I don't deserve this treatment from you."

59

Not once in twenty-eight chapters did Job ever ask, "Lord, what am I supposed to do in light of these circumstances?" All he accomplished was to make himself bitter at God, frustrated with himself, and earned himself a stinging rebuke from God. All of which could have been avoided if he had just had the right perspective. It is not my intention to be overly critical of Job, after all, he did go through a terrible trial. But how much mental anguish might have been avoided if he had just asked the right question? He looked at his past and present life and saw no purpose for the current situation, so he justified himself instead of justifying God. He started off not charging God foolishly, but it didn't last long; time and "friends" did the Devil's work. Charging God foolishly was exactly what he ended up doing.

Job was frustrated because there was nothing he could do about any of his circumstances. He could not fix his health, wealth, family, or reputation; and he could see no reason for God allowing this in his life. The one thing Job could have controlled was his attitude, and it is the one thing he never accomplished. He had the perfect opportunity to declare his trust in a righteous God, regardless of his circumstances; and, instead, he declared his own righteousness. He blew the opportunity to accomplish the one thing that was in his control.

Yes, Job was rewarded in the end; but not until he received a stinging rebuke in front of his friends. Job was rewarded because God is faithful and had no major cause to afflict Job the way He did (Job 2:3). But I can't help but wonder how much more reward Job might have received if he had kept his attitude right and justified God instead of himself.

60

Job never asked the "what" or "why" questions, but he got the answer to "what" when God did what Job should have done: glorified Himself in front of all of them.

How many of us would have liked to have gagged our children when they started the "why" series? It sometimes seemed like the only word they had in their vocabulary was "why."

It goes something like this:

Mom: Eat your green beans, honey.

Child: Why?

Mom: Because you need them.

Child: Why?

Mom: Because they'll make you grow big and strong.

Child: Why?

Mom: BECAUSE I SAID SO!

Is it just childish curiosity that causes them to ask why; or does it stem from an inherent lack of trust?

Is it wrong to ask God "why"? I would say it all depends on your motive. Does the question come from a real desire to know and correct something that may be wrong in your life? Or is the question driven from a lack of trust? Or from an exalted self-opinion that doesn't think it deserves this kind of treatment? The first motive would be acceptable; the others would not. A better question to ask is "what" instead of "why."

Now, all that being said, let me give you the other part to the equation; one which you will also not appreciate, perhaps even more than the "why" explanation. Sometimes even the "what" question will not get an answer from the Lord. Not nearly as often as "why," but it will still happen.

Look at the situation with the Nation of Israel wandering in the wilderness. I'm sure there were times when they had questions about, "What are we doing here?" They are an exception to what I said about "why." The answer to that question was the fact that they were being punished for their disobedience of not going into the Promised Land as the Lord told them. They knew the answer to "why." But I'm sure they had the "what" question when the Lord parked them in their encampment for a year at a time. Sometimes they were encamped for a day, sometimes a week or month, and sometimes a year and possibly more. So there they sat with nothing to do except tend to their animals, and I'm sure they asked many times, "what are we doing here?" And the answer was? Nothing! There was no answer to that question for them. The answer for them was found in the answer to the "why" question. You are doing nothing, and are not going to do anything, until you learn not to disobey God!

Wouldn't the ultimate test of our faith be that we continue to trust Him, even when God doesn't give us the answers to either "why" or "what," and just lets us wander in the wilderness? Would that not be a great test of faith? Would that not make our faith stronger when deliverance did come?

Brethren, the question of "why" is a reactive question, but the question of "what" is a proactive one. One is defensive and one is offensive. Let us all strive not to live our lives on the defense but on the offense. Whether we get an answer or not, do we not belong to a God that loves us beyond our capacity to understand? Has He not promised to supply all our need, never leave or forsake us, and take all our care upon His own shoulders? Then why can't we just leave it at that? Why can't we just say, "God, I know you are in control of my life, and I'll trust you no matter what you do or allow!" God help us all to reach that kind of high ground in our lives. Search for the answer to "what?" Yes, certainly do; there most likely will be something He wants us to learn. But if we get no answer, let the words of this song sink into our hearts:

> Trust and obey
> For there's no other way
> To be happy in Jesus
> But to trust and obey.
>
> John H. Simms, Daniel B Towner

Finally, one more thing to remember: God's greatest works are done in deep waters. In Luke 5:1-8 we read that Peter and his partners had been fishing all night and caught nothing. And then the Lord showed up, preached His sermon, and then told Peter to "launch out into the deep." The result was the greatest catch of fish they had ever had, to the point where Peter knew something extraordinary had taken place, and he fell at the feet of Jesus. If the Lord takes you through deep waters, it is for His glory, and your benefit. The results will be worth it!

Chapter Seven: Prayer - A first Resort, Not A Last One

"To seek aid in time of distress from a supernatural Being is an instinct of human nature. I believe in the truthfulness of this instinct, and that man prays because there is something in prayer. As when the Creator gives His creature the power of thirst, it is because water exists to meet its thirst; and as when He creates hunger there is food to correspond to the appetite; so when He inclines men to pray it is because prayer has a corresponding blessing connected with it." -C. H. Spurgeon

Robert Murray M'Cheyne, one of the world's great Christians, said: "If the veil of the world's machinery were lifted off, how much we would find is done in answer to the prayers of God's children."[2]

There is an amazing passage of scripture found in Exodus 32:1-14. Moses was on Mount Sinai for forty days with God; and while he was gone, the people had corrupted themselves, made a golden calf to worship, and were having a very godless party to celebrate their new found "freedom." In verses 9-10 the Lord makes an amazing statement. He says, "…let me alone,…" He was telling Moses NOT to pray for the people because God wanted to destroy them. In other words, "Don't hinder me, Moses, I have something I want to do, and I don't

---

[2] Andrew A. Bonar, *The Biography of Robert Murray M'Cheyne*, (Zondervan Publishing House, Grand Rapids, MI, Kindle edition), location 1659.

want you stopping me!" God telling a man not to hinder Him? The implication is that prayer opens or closes a door in order for God to work, or not work, on someone's behalf by reasoning with God about what is best, which is exactly what Moses did. He brought God's reputation and promises to His remembrance, and God couldn't argue with the reasoning.

We see the same principle in effect in the New Testament when the Lord Jesus was dealing with the Syrophenician woman in Mark 7. She was a foreigner who wanted the Lord's help, and He told her to forget it because He was only there to help the Jews. But she was able to take His words, combined with great humility, and turn them against Him by pure reason, so that He was unable to ignore her prayer request. "Yes, Lord, I'm a dog, but even the dogs eat the crumbs under the master's table." He would have appeared unreasonable and uncaring to all those around Him if He had not helped her. After all, didn't He tell us to come and reason with Him in Isaiah 1:18? How could He tell us to reason with Him and then not be reasonable Himself?

Brethren, prayer allows God to do something He would not normally do in a certain circumstance. God certainly *could* have consumed the Jews without help or permission if He wanted to. He could have gone right ahead with His planned judgment and been perfectly justified in doing so. But He knows Moses is about to plead for the people with good resasoning, and He didn't want Moses making any good excuses for them that would stop Him from His planned action.

So the question is: what is God's planned action for us, and will He allow us to change it? Can we pray with fervency and sound reasoning in order to be effective in changing God's mind (James 5:16)? The scriptural basis is yes; at times we can. And I believe with certainty that is what God allowed in at least one instance when I was struggling for life after coming home from the hospital.

After receiving Interferon treatments for seven months, and the virus mutating and beating the treatment, I was told there was nothing more they could do for me. My liver functions began getting worse, but instead of continuing that way, they started fluctuating up and down. One week they would be too high, and the next week they would be back down. That trend continues to this day. None of us were ever sure whether I was going to live or die. But all during my time in the hospital and post surgery treatment, I had been telling people what a great God I served, and about the miracles He had performed on my behalf. Now I was faced with the prospect of dying, and I was seriously bothered by the fact that people (especially unsaved people) would have an opportunity to discount, or totally disbelieve, what I had told them about the things God had done for me. I was worried about them giving up the hope it had generated in them, and was also worried about God's reputation. The prospect of dying in itself did not bother or worry me. I know I'm a saved man and my eternal home is in Heaven with the Lord. But I was concerned for the people around me, and the exaltation I had given the Lord being written off as just fanaticism. I was also concerned for Pam being left behind if the Lord took me home. So I prayed earnestly that God would allow me to live, or at least would not allow people to lose faith and hope if He did take me home. And I continue to pray this to this day as a testimony of God's grace and the power of earnest prayer. Not that I am a great prayer warrior, or a particularly righteous man, because I certainly am not. But through humility and reason I believe God changed His mind about taking me home at that time. Once again, it shows the greatness of the God I love.

Another example of our ability to reason with the Lord and change His mind is found in Genesis 18 where God sends two of His angels to destroy Sodom. His plan was to destroy the entire population because of their wickedness. We know that God is not willing that any should perish (2 Peter 3:9), but the sin of the people demanded the wrath of God be executed upon them. The fact that He really didn't want to destroy the people is brought out by the fact that He told Abraham what He was about to do. God didn't have to inform Abraham of His plan; but even in a situation of perverseness and total ungodliness, God's compassion still moved Him to inform people of His plan, most likely in the hope that someone would act exactly as Abraham did.

Abraham reasoned with God that it would not be a righteous thing to do if He were to destroy the righteous along with the wicked. He made the statement: "shall not the Judge of all the earth do right?" That statement moved God to rethink His plan. Notice also Abraham's humility in verse 32. Abraham was most likely trying to save Lot, his children, and their families; However, he pleaded for the entire city and not just his own family. His reasoning, combined with his compassion was, I believe, something with which the Lord could not argue. Unfortunately, the Lord must not have found ten righteous people in the city and His original plan was implemented. But if the Lord *had* found ten, the city would have been spared through the prayers and intercession of one man, Abraham.

Brethren, God's mind can sometimes be changed. Perhaps His plan for you is not set in concrete. And if not, are you willing to continue in fervent, humble prayer to see if you can change His mind? What does the word <u>fervent</u> mean? It means passionate, heated, and intense. Fervent prayer, then, would mean there are going to be times when you are going to have to have a knock down, drag out with God. You will have to put away all piety and false pretenses, and reason with Him as you would any other person, but with humility and respect. Tell God exactly what is in your heart; He knows what is there anyway, so you might as well be honest and don't put on any airs. If you do not take your prayers seriously, neither will God. Don't be afraid, it is what He commanded us to do in James.

There is also one other qualifier to the formula: are you willing to accept His answer, *with thanksgiving, if He doesn't change His mind*? Will you embrace the cross He has set before you with love, trust, and confidence in His perfect will? If so, then there is a real possibility of you joining the ranks of men like Moses and Abraham that changed the mind of God.

> 1Th 5:18 "In <u>every thing</u> give thanks: for this is the will of God in Christ Jesus concerning you."

Brethren, in John 15:5 the Lord tells us:

> "I am the vine, ye are the branches: He that abideth in me, and I in him, the same bringeth forth much fruit: for without me ye can do nothing."

"Without me ye can do nothing!" In order for us to accomplish anything in God's will, or ever change His mind, we are going to have to *abide* in Him, and *pray earnestly*. I have seen God answer prayers in my own life after praying and waiting for twenty-five years! Never stop praying until you receive an answer you are sure is from Him, whether it is what you had hoped for or not. He may just be testing your seriousness in getting the answer, or testing your faithfulness to do as you are commanded.

There are times, however, when you may have found that all the praying, crying, and fervency doesn't seem to affect God. It seems there are times when God doesn't give you an answer one way or another. Is there a reason He is compelled to treat us in such a seemingly uncaring manner? Allow me to give you a few reasons as to the possible cause. Since this is not a book about prayer, I will only give you a brief outline of a few reasons, and you will have to do your own homework for the rest. God doesn't always answer prayer when:

1. Family relations between a husband and wife are not right (1 Peter 3:5-7).
2. Your relations with the brethren are not right (Zec 7:9-11,13).
3. There is personal sin you won't deal with. (Isa 59:1-2).

Brethren, live as clean a life as you can, seek God fervently, seek Godly counsel, make prayer your first option instead of the last, and watch God do miraculous things.

Chapter Eight: God's Sovereignty

1Co 6:19-20 "What? know ye not that your body is the temple of the Holy Ghost which is in you, which ye have of God, and ye are not your own? For ye are bought with a price: therefore glorify God in your body, and in your spirit, which are God's."

This subject is one that is difficult for many to accept, and also for someone to write, teach, or preach about. It deals with one of the ways of God that seems hard or brutal at times. But, in reality, it only seems that way to us because we do not see God the way He truly is. My hope it that you will pray and think about this doctrine and see that it is just as pure and right as any in the word of God.

There may be some of you reading this that have, at times, thought, or even said, that God has no right to do this thing, whatever it may be. After all, Lord, haven't I been a good person? Haven't I tried my best to be what you want me to be? Haven't I given my life to your service? Do we ask the same question Peter asked when he said, "Behold, we have forsaken all, and followed thee; what shall we have therefore?" Is that not a normal, human response? Are not people's lives based on performance and reward? Don't we work hard on the job only to expect a salary and/or position increase? Are there many of us that are not prone to desire recognition, praise, and reward for our hard work, both in the secular and spiritual worlds? That is, and always has been, the philosophy of the entire world. And truly, God does reward faithful service, as His response to Peter's question shows –

Mr 10:30 "But he shall receive an hundredfold now in this time, houses, and brethren, and sisters, and mothers, and children, and lands, with persecutions; and in the world to come eternal life."

However, as Christians, that is not supposed to be our motive. Our motive for serving Jesus Christ is supposed to one of love, honor, loyalty, and duty. These are noble motives that deserve our utmost commitment every moment of every day of our lives.

Lu 17:10 "So likewise ye, when ye shall have done all those things which are commanded you, say, We are unprofitable servants: we have done that which was our duty to do."

Notice there is nothing self-serving in that verse at all. We serve because we are expected to, and because we love the One that commands it. Serving from a sense of *duty, loyalty,* and *honor* is a quality at which many people today would openly laugh. You would indeed be called a fool by many for stating that your desire to serve was based solely on those things. You would probably even be called a liar by many, so far removed is the concept from today's society.

But it was not always this way. We have only to look in the pages of our Bible to find, time and time again, service to God and His people based not on greed or reward, but on the three things listed above. Look at David's men in 1 Chron. 11 when David longed for a drink of water from the well in Bethlehem. Three men hazarded their lives by breaking through the defenses of the army of the Philistines, made their way to the well, drew the water, and then had to make their way back through an army that knew they were there! What was their motivation for doing so? Only one: love for the man that was their leader and sovereign. There wasn't even duty involved in this; just pure love. It was "above and beyond the call of duty."

Just look at the life and motive of Moses, a Jew by birth, but raised as the son of Pharaoh. All the wealth and power of Egypt lay at his feet. All he had to do was keep his mouth shut as to his heritage and all would be available to him. But what was his response?

Heb 11:24-27 "By faith Moses, when he was come to years, refused to be called the son of Pharaoh's daughter; Choosing rather to suffer affliction with the people of God, than to enjoy the pleasures of sin for a season; Esteeming the reproach of Christ greater riches than the treasures in Egypt: for he had respect unto the recompence of the reward. By faith he forsook Egypt, not fearing the wrath of the king: for he endured, as seeing him who is invisible."

What is the reward spoken of in the verse? It is answered for us in the verses themselves, "Esteeming the reproach of Christ greater riches than the treasures of

Egypt..." Once again, love is driving a person to drastic measures; but this time it is coupled with a sense of duty to his people, and to the God that loves those people.

Why did the Apostle Paul give up the wealth of being a lawyer and Pharisee? Why did he willing submit to being beaten, shipwrecked, imprisoned, and in his own words: *"endure the loss of all things?"* Duty, honor, loyalty, and love, for a sovereign God who also endured seeing His greatest treasure, His Son, suffer terribly on behalf of others. Paul as well, did it for the Lord Jesus Christ who endured the loss of all things because of His love for us, and His duty toward a holy and sovereign God.

The thought that "God has no right to do this; I've been a good and faithful servant, why are you doing this to me;" may be an appropriate question, at times, for an employer, spouse, child, or other human being. But it is not an appropriate question for the Lord. As I have stated earlier, the Lord does nothing arbitrarily or to no purpose. He always has a reason for everything that He does, and I have endeavored to help you see what some of those reasons are.

But even more than that, I think you can see from the verses in 1 Corinthians 6, that if you are a Born Again Christian you have been bought and paid for by the precious blood of the Lord Jesus Christ, and you no longer belong to yourself. Notice the verses say "ye are not your own..." So many people (I would have to be so bold and say the majority of "Christians") ask the Lord to save them from the fires of Hell, but then continue living their lives according to their own dictates. This is not God's plan for you. His plan for you is, "...*therefore glorify God in your body, and in your spirit, which are God's.*" The kind of thinking that makes a person say "God has no right" is the kind of thinking that will not get you the blessings of God. Instead, you may find that you receive a rebuke. Not only that, but think of what the alternative would have been had you not been Born Again. You might be thinking, "I never would have received Christ as my Savior if I had known what God was going to expect of me." Are you saying then that the Lake of Fire would really have been a better choice? Again you may say, "But God gets His way in either decision I make." Correct, and He has that right! Brethren, our God is not a God that took over from some other god's work and just laid down His own set of rules on someone else's creation. He is our Creator, and as such, He created us for His pleasure. He has a sovereign right to dictate our lives as He sees best.

Rev 4.11 "Thou art worthy, O Lord, to receive glory and honour and power: for thou hast created all things, and for thy pleasure they are and were created."

Brethren, our God is truly a marvelous being, and nothing we ever give or do for Him is too much. Sit down in prayerful meditation sometime and try thinking about what God is, and what you would say to someone when trying to explain God to them.

If you were to say "God is great," would that do justice to the true nature of God? Does that statement explain the fullness of the Godhead? What if you said, "God is love." Would that fully explain Him? You would be leaving out the wrath of God, the grace, patience, longsuffering, kindness, charity, and a host of His other attributes.

How can we, as finite beings, wrap our minds around an infinite Being that has no beginning or end, no sin, and no need of anything? He is completely self-sustaining. If you were going to try to explain God properly, you would have to use His own words to do so; words that are both vague, and yet explain Him fully at the same time: "*I am that I am,*" (Ex. 3:14). What else could God, or anyone else, say about Him that wouldn't fall short in some way?

Our creator is Omnipotent, Omniscient, and Omnipresent. Explain it? There's no way to explain it. We just have to accept it. The same way we have to accept the fact that we are His creation made solely for His pleasure, and our job in this life is to find out what His will for us is and accomplish it. Does He have the right to do with us as He sees fit, regardless of our desires?

Let's say, as an example, that you work with your hands in some way: wood working, sewing, baking, etc. You make something for a specific purpose, and the object doesn't work for the purpose for which you designed it. Do you not have the right to destroy it in some manner? Is it not your creation that took your time, effort, and money to make? Certainly, that is your right. And just because we are living beings, does that negate God's sovereignty over His creation? No, my friend, it does not. Not only does God have the right to do with us what He will because He bought us with His own blood, He has the right because He created us. And He created us for a specific purpose which, if we don't fulfill, and God allows us to continue in life, just shows what a gracious, loving, and long-suffering God He really is. But if He allows sorrow and tragedy to come into our lives, it

78

is because He only wants to make us better vessels "meet for the Master's use." We need to learn to rejoice in that, instead of blaming Him for allowing something in our lives that we don't like. Look at the following verse.

> *Rom 9.20-21 "Nay but, O man, who art thou that repliest against God? Shall the thing formed say to him that formed it, Why hast thou made me thus? Hath not the potter power over the clay, of the same lump to make one vessel unto honour, and another unto dishonour?"*

Brethren, I don't mean or want to be hard on anyone. Please remember that I look into a mirror as well as a computer monitor as I write these things. I sometimes don't like what I'm saying anymore than some of you do right now. However, we must remember that we do not set the terms of our service and life's purpose, God does. If that is a repugnant thought to you, then you should have read the contract a little more thoroughly before signing it. Once you said–I receive and accept the Lord Jesus Christ as my Savior, the contract is signed in blood. The terms are set: you are not your own, you are bought with a price.

God, why are you doing this to me? Because He has every right to do so as your owner. *You gave Him that permission and power over you.* Now it is time to go back to the chapter on "From Why to What" and read it again.

"Why" - because He has a perfect right to.

"What" – because He does have a perfect plan for you. And if you learn to embrace that as a gift from a loving, caring, all-knowing and all-powerful God and friend, you will find it is not as repugnant as you thought; but the true and only way to the peace, joy, and fulfilling life He has promised you.

If the Lord decides that your life will better serve and bring glory to Him if He allows tragedy to come into your life, and stay with you the rest of your life, what will your response be? God has performed many true miracles in my life in the last two years in keeping me alive. However, if He decides that I can bring more glory to Him by remaining sick, than in being healed, what are my choices? Simple: backslide and fall away from the life God has planned for me, or follow on. And it all comes down to chapter one: "I'm Still Trusting My Lord." So let me ask you, "Are you still trusting Him? Does He really still love you?" Or do you believe the lies of Satan when he tells you that God is punishing you and doesn't care about you; that God is an evil task master Who only wants His way; that He doesn't love you anymore, so why continue serving such a cruel God; or any of the other lies Satan is prone to put in your ear. Brethren, we cannot stop him from putting those things in our ears; but we don't have to let them into our hearts and control our actions.

Pr 4:23 "Keep thy heart with all diligence; for out of it are the issues of life."

One major thing we must keep in perspective in regards to healing and the glory of God is the whole purpose of healing. As Henry Frost points out in his excellent book *Miraculous Healing,*[3] Christ's main purpose in healing people was not His compassion on them, although compassion was certainly a factor. It was, however, not the principle factor. If compassion had been the principle factor, then why was Christ so selective in those He healed in any particular town or village? How many sick people were in Jerusalem at the time of Christ's healing of the man at the Pool of Bethesda? Indeed, how many other people were at the pool that day that Christ evidently paid no attention to at all? One man only received the healing touch of the Great Physician. Are we to assume that Christ had no compassion on the rest of those that had waited years to be healed? How many people were at the grave site of Lazarus, who also had family buried in the same graveyard, hoping Christ would do for their loved one what He did for Lazarus? Did Christ have no compassion on them? Certainly, He had compassion on them all; but only one was healed, and one was raised from the dead. Then it must be concluded that the primary factor in healing was not His compassion on them, but His glorification and reputation among the people. Notice what He tells the disciples about the situation with Lazarus:

Jn 11:4 *"When Jesus heard that, he said, This sickness is not unto death, but for the glory of God, that the Son of God might be glorified thereby."*

[3] Henry Frost, *Miraculous Healing,* (Christian Focus Publications Ltd., Geanies House, Fearn, Ross-shire, Scotland, UK 2008) p. 102.

Christ raised Lazarus for *His* glory, not for the benefit of Lazarus. Lazarus would eventually come up from the dead at the resurrection, just as Martha had stated. That was not the issue. The issue was Christ's glory. Indeed, bringing someone back to earth to live and die again, that had just been in heaven for four days, is not exactly what I would call an act of compassion! If Lazarus had his choice, he probably would have opted to stay in heaven and wait for his body until later.

We see the same principle applied in John 9 with the healing of the blind man.

> Jn 9:1-5 *"And as Jesus passed by, he saw a man which was blind from his birth. And his disciples asked him, saying, Master, who did sin, this man, or his parents, that he was born blind? Jesus answered, Neither hath this man sinned, nor his parents: but that the works of God should be made manifest in him. I must work the works of him that sent me, while it is day: the night cometh, when no man can work. As long as I am in the world, I am the light of the world."*

The purpose of the healing did not come primarily from Christ's compassion on the man, but on the basis of showing the world who the Light of the world was.

Now, lest you think that to be an egotistical reason for healing, allow me to remind you of the fact that one day, all who have put their trust in Jesus Christ as their Savior, will be healed. His compassion eventually brings healing to us all; but even then, will we just take the healing, say thank you, and be on our merry way? Or will we fall at the feet of Jesus, and cast our crowns at His feet as our Sovereign? The ultimate factor is still the glory of God.

Once again imagine the people standing by when Christ healed the man at the pool. What were their thoughts when one man was healed and they were passed by? Did they rejoice in the power and glory of God? Were they happy for the one that did receive the healing, or were they envious, bitter, and mad that they were not recipients of the same blessing? Whose ego is really in question here? Are not our heart's true motives revealed to us at times like that, just as Job's was? So what will our reaction be when we are passed over for healing in this life? Will we rejoice over those who have been healed, or will we be bitter, and doubt God's love for us, because we were not. Or, if we do receive the healing touch, will Christ be able to use us for the purpose He healed us for: to bring glory and honor to Him; or will we just take the healing, say thank you, and go about our daily lives according to our own dictates?

It is easy at times, especially times of severe illness or other tragedy, for us to believe that God doesn't love or care for us. Let me answer that with this illustration.

I recently read a book called "The Cross And The Swastika."[4] If you want to read a book about the love of God, without reading a book specifically about the love of God, then this is a great book to read. It is about a U.S. Army Chaplain, Henry Gerecke, at the end of WWII. He became the Chaplain of Spandau Military Prison where

---

[4] F.T. Grossmith, *The Cross And The Swastika,* (Pacific Press Publishing Association, Oshawa, Ontario, Canada, 1989).

all the Nazi hierarchy were kept after the Nuremberg trials. He had many opportunities to witness about the love of God and Salvation in Jesus Christ to men like Rudolph Hess, Herman Goering, Reich Minister Von Ribbentrop, Admiral and Reich's President Karl Donitz, Field Marshal Heinz Guderian, and Deputy Fuehrer Heinrich Himmler before he killed himself. He was actually able to lead several of these men to Christ for salvation, including Albert Speer, Von Ribbentrop, Donitz, and Guderian. Now keep in mind what these men had just done to the *"apple of his eye,"* Deuteronomy 32:10. They murdered, tortured, raped, and finally burned in the ovens over six million of God's chosen people. Now keep in mind also the love, instead of hatred, God put in Gerecke's own heart that allowed him to witness to these men, in spite of the fact that two of his own sons had been badly wounded while fighting these same people. And still God loved those men enough, in spite of their sin, to send someone to them, and to actually save some of them!

How can any of us ever doubt the love and compassion that God has for you and me? That is a lie the Devil wants us to believe, and he will go to extraordinary lengths to try to convince us of it so that we will quit on the God that did not quit on us. Brethren, when God allows things to happen to us that we don't like or understand, it is because of some great purpose He has for us that for some unknown reason He cannot reveal to us at that time. And remember this verse that I wrote in an earlier chapter; it is one of my favorites.

Pr 23:18 "For surely there is an end; and thine expectation shall not be cut off."

Here are a few more verses for you to consider concerning this subject:

Isa 46:5-11 "To whom will ye liken me, and make me equal, and compare me, that we may be like? They lavish gold out of the bag, and weigh silver in the balance, and hire a goldsmith; and he maketh it a god: they fall down, yea, they worship. They bear him upon the shoulder, they carry him, and set him in his place, and he standeth; from his place shall he not remove: yea, one shall cry unto him, yet can he not answer, nor save him out of his trouble. Remember this, and shew yourselves men: bring it again to mind, O ye transgressors. Remember the former things of old: for I am God, and there is none else; I am God, and there is none like me, Declaring the end from the beginning, and from ancient times the things that are not yet done, saying, My counsel shall stand, and I will do all my pleasure: Calling a ravenous bird from the east, the man that executeth my counsel from a far country: yea, I have spoken it, I will also bring it to pass; I have purposed it, I will also do it."

✞

Jer 18.6 "O house of Israel, cannot I do with you as this potter? saith the LORD. Behold, as the clay is in the potter's hand, so are ye in mine hand, O house of Israel."

✝

Pr 25:2 "It is the glory of God to conceal a thing: but the honour of kings is to search out a matter."

✝

Brethren, never forget that "God is love" (1 John 4:8). And the love He has for us is off the scale of our understanding and reasoning. But He is also sovereign, and deserves, and demands, our complete and total obedience in every area of our lives. That obedience is pleasing to God.

Chapter Nine: A Loving Father

Ps 103:13 "Like as a father pitieth his children, so the LORD pitieth them that fear him."

Pr 3:12 "For whom the LORD loveth he correcteth; even as a father the son in whom he delighteth."

Ps 22:24-25 "For he hath not despised nor abhorred the affliction of the afflicted; neither hath he hid his face from him; but when he cried unto him, he heard. My praise shall be of thee in the great congregation: 1 will pay my vows before them that fear him."

In our "Fight For Light" we must always be on guard for anything that our flesh, other people, or the Devil will bring into our lives that will take away from the supremacy of God in all things. They will try to make us bitter or distrusting, or in some other way low-rate God in our hearts. After talking about the *sovereignty* of God, we also need to look at the doctrine of God as our loving, kind, and merciful Father; someone who wants only the best for our lives, but who also knows that the best thing we can ever do with our lives is live them according to His ways. Look with me at the following verse:

Jn 10.10 "The thief cometh not, but for to steal, and to kill, and to destroy: 1 am come that they might have life, and that they might have it more abundantly."

What a tremendous statement! The promise from the Lord is an abundant life, and one more abundant than anything the world has to offer. And just like any good father wants a closer relationship with his children, so the Lord wants a close relationship with us. However, sometimes it takes a tragedy to motivate us to want that kind of relationship because we have a sneaky suspicion from reading our Bible that the kind of relationship God wants is one that is going to cost us something to attain; and we are afraid of what that cost might be.

I remember as a young Christian walking into my first pastor's office to talk to him about that very thing. I had just attended my first revival meeting, and I realized that the men who were preaching had something in their lives that I desperately needed. I had seen an authority, assuredness, and purpose in their lives that I did not possess. I told my pastor that very thing and he looked at me with all solemnity and said, "You can have it, but it will cost you something." I remember saying, "Well, I don't know if I can pay it or not, but I'm willing to try." And now, after thirty years, and knowing something of the cost, I realize now more than ever what a great, loving, and merciful God I have as my Father, and that no cost is too high to pay for the privilege of having a close relationship with Him.

But rest assured, you will find Him peculiar in His dealings with man. Let me give you a few examples if I may. In Luke 24.13-31 we find the story of the disciples on the road to Emmaus. The Lord came up and walked with them, but hid His identity from them. When it was His will to walk and fellowship with them, why then did He hide Himself from them? Especially after he had preached to them along the way about Himself, and the prophecies concerning Him, why did He then act like He didn't want to be with them? When they arrived at their destination, vs. 28 says the Lord "*made as though he would have gone further."* In our terms He said: see you fellows later, I'm going to move on down the road a bit. But they kept asking Him to come in with them, and He finally acquiesced and went in. He truly wanted their companionship and fellowship; but, more importantly, He wanted to see how serious they were about fellowshipping with Him, and their learning more about the One that they thought had been the Christ. It was a test; one which, if they had failed, would have cost them the revelation of His being alive and of seeing His miracle first hand.

His ways are as unchangeable today as they were back then. He still tests us to see if we really want His presence in our lives. We see this same thing occuring in other places in the gospels; places where it almost seems the Lord is trying to turn away followers instead of encouraging them to follow. He is not only very unpleasant, but sometimes is even offensive to people that come to him. Look at the following verses and tell me the Lord wasn't testing these young men's resolve to follow Him by the way He talked to them.

Lu 9:57-62 "And it came to pass, that, as they went in the way, a certain man said unto him, Lord, I will follow thee whithersoever thou goest. And Jesus said unto him, Foxes have holes, and birds of the air have nests; but the Son of man hath not where to lay his head. And he said unto another, Follow me. But he said, Lord, suffer me first to go and bury my father. Jesus said unto him, Let the dead bury their dead: but go thou and preach the kingdom of God. And another also

> said, Lord, I will follow thee; but let me first go bid them
> farewell, which are at home at my house. And Jesus said unto
> him, No man, having put his hand to the plough, and looking
> back, is fit for the kingdom of God."

What kind of a way is that to talk to people? These were reasonable requests, but the Lord answers them so roughly that it is not recorded that any of them ever followed Him. Would you have followed Him; would I? We have a saying, "There is no wound like the wound of a friend." But in reality, how many of us would have said, "Ok, Lord, I'll miss my father's funeral", or, "Ok, Lord, my family doesn't need to know why I suddenly disappeared!" Not many of us. And yet, knowing the love of God, if they had taken the rebuff and followed Him, He would surely have stopped, granted their requests, and waited for them. This is one of the Lord's ways that we can never hope to fully understand, but His test worked. They were "fair weather" friends and I'm sure He knew it. Fair weather friends are only exposed for what they are in bad weather or in the threat of it. But, as with the disciples on the Sea of Galilee, those that follow on experience the miracle of the Lord turning bad weather into perfect calm. And what He can do in nature, He is much more capable of doing in our hearts, minds, and lives.

None of us would ever willingly choose to be chronically ill. Which of us would not rather have our health the way it used to be? It's revealing how our perspectives change when sickness, injury, or some other debilitating problem comes along and limits how we live our lives. I now miss being able to do things I used to hate! Even the dreaded task of shoveling snow, I would now rejoice over if I were able to do it. However, my muscles are completely gone, I've lost 50 lbs. of body weight, and when I tried to throw a tennis ball for my dog yesterday, it flew about 12 feet. This from someone who used to snow and water ski, play tennis, work out with free weights, preach and teach in several prisons and jails, teach in our church's Bible institute, ride a bike, and many other things.

I did not choose to be sick; but it is my choice how I handle the emotional and spiritual side of this trial. I must choose to Fight For Light, and to trust and follow God or give up as Job's wife encouraged him to do.

Do I chose to believe that God is working this out to my benefit, the benefit of those around me, and to His glory? Do I believe that He truly is a loving Father?

Php 1:6 "Being confident of this very thing, that he which hath begun a good work in you will perform it until the day of Jesus Christ:"

Do I chose to believe that an all-powerful, all-loving and compassionate God is going to work this out for good like Romans 8 says He will? Do I chose to believe that it is the *inward* man, not the *outward* man that is the important part of us, and that if we allow God to accomplish His will that it will be worth it all one day? Do I choose to believe what I have been taught all my Christian life, that my personal relationship with Jesus Christ is more important than any other aspect of

Christianity? Do I choose to believe that my Father is acting in my best interest? It is all totally my decision.

> 2Co 4:16-18 *"For which cause we faint not; but though our outward man perish, yet the inward man is renewed day by day. For our light affliction, which is but for a moment, worketh for us a far more exceeding and eternal weight of glory; While we look not at the things which are seen, but at the things which are not seen: for the things which are seen are temporal; but the things which are not seen are eternal."*

Our *light* affliction? How can Paul say that? Because compared to what my Father ordained His Son to do on my behalf at Calvary, it is a very light affliction indeed.

Dr. David Jeremiah, in his book *A Bend in the Road* says:

> "Here is the truth you must fully comprehend and stake your life upon if you remember no other words from this chapter: He turned His back upon His Son so that He would never have to turn His back on you. That was the excruciating price He paid because He loves you that much. He lived and died and suffered on this earth so you wouldn't have to he [sic] forsaken."[5]

---

[5] David Jeremiah, *A Bend in the Road,* (W Publishing Group, a division of Thomas Nelson Inc., Nashville, TN 37214, 2000, Kindle edition), loc. 1065.

Do I chose to believe what Paul says in 2 Cor. 12, even if I can't see it right now, or do I choose to believe he's crazy and doesn't know what he's saying?

2Co 12:7-10 "And lest I should be exalted above measure through the abundance of the revelations, there was given to me a thorn in the flesh, the messenger of Satan to buffet me, lest I should be exalted above measure. For this thing I besought the Lord thrice, that it might depart from me. And he said unto me, My grace is sufficient for thee: for my strength is made perfect in weakness. Most gladly therefore will I rather glory in my infirmities, that the power of Christ may rest upon me. Therefore I take pleasure in infirmities, in reproaches, in necessities, in persecutions, in distresses for Christ's sake: for when I am weak, then am I strong."

✝

Do I trust and love God enough as my loving Father to believe that what He did for Paul in those verses He can and will do for me?

The final question is: Do I chose God? Do I really trust Him? Will I honestly say what the Lord Jesus Christ said in His darkest hour, "FATHER, if it be possible let this cup pass from me, nevertheless, NOT MY WILL BUT THINE BE DONE?"

So many times I've heard people say, "I'm just bearing my cross!" As if it were a great unbearable trial for them. I'm not making light of carrying your cross, that's what the Lord told us to do. And carrying it does take faith and trust on our part. But carrying the cross is not the end of the Via Dolorosa. The end of the way is at Calvary, and being *nailed to that cross*. It is dying to ourselves, and living unto God (a subject I will deal with in a later chapter). Will you say, as Christ said, and as I have also said along the way of this illness, "My God, My God, why hast thou forsaken me?"

Had God forsaken His Son? NO! But in the midst of the terrible trial, it seemed to Christ that He was all alone, abandoned by friends, mocked by His enemies, and abandoned by God. It is also my choice whether or not to finish my course the way He did, by trusting my Father even though it looks as if I am forsaken. At the end of His terrible trial, in Luke 23:46 Jesus said, "...Father, into thy hands I commend my spirit: and having said thus, he gave up the ghost."

Regardless of the circumstances or how things appeared, He trusted God to the end. I did not choose to be sick, but I choose to trust my Father's care and plan for my life. Do I also choose to embrace and use this experience for God and others, or will I wallow in my own self-pity? Please allow me to quote an important verse once again -

Rev 4.11 "Thou art worthy, O Lord, to receive glory and honour and power: for thou hast created all things, and for thy pleasure they are and were created."

And one more great verse to help boost your spirits -

Jer 29.11 "For I know the thoughts that I think toward you, saith the LORD, thoughts of peace, and not of evil, to give you an expected end."

Allow me to give you one more example before I leave this section; a personal one that some of you may be able to relate to. There have been some very special times that I have enjoyed over the years with my sons, and with Pam. How much I have enjoyed the company of them when, from time to time, I have been off to run some mundane errand, and they have asked to come along. I have often told them, "I'm not going any place special," and they have answered me saying, "That's ok, I just want to spend time with you." If you've never known that experience, I pity you; it is truly one of life's great moments.

How it must please God when we ask to simply be with Him for fellowship, when we know that His path will lead us through deep and troubled waters. I try to make it a practice in my prayer life that on Wednesday mornings I don't ask God for anything. I review the events of the prior week, and just thank and praise Him for what He's done for me. I feel like such a beggar sometimes when I'm always going to God with my hand out for something; therefore, I take one day just to tell Him I love Him, and not ask for a thing. He does so many things to show His love for me; I think it's only right to reciprocate in kind. Try it, you'll like it!

The Fight For Light

Chapter Ten: The Fight For Light -The Great Battle With Self

1Ti 6:12 "Fight the good fight of faith, lay hold on eternal life, whereunto thou art also called, and hast professed a good profession before many witnesses."

Eph 6:10-13 "Finally, my brethren, be strong in the Lord, and in the power of his might. Put on the whole armour of God, that ye may be able to stand against the wiles of the devil. For we wrestle not against flesh and blood, but against principalities, against powers, against the rulers of the darkness of this world, against spiritual wickedness in high places. Wherefore take unto you the whole armour of God, that ye may be able to withstand in the evil day, <u>and having done all, to stand.</u>"

I once heard about a poster that showed a little boy in a baseball uniform, sitting with his hat and glove on the ground, hands hanging down between his knees, and who was obviously very dejected at having done poorly in the game. The caption at the top read, "I quit." In the bottom right hand corner of the poster was another small picture. It was of Calvary, and the cross of our Lord. The caption on it read, "I didn't."

In our Christian walk, warfare is, unfortunately, something that we will engage in until the Lord finally calls us home. It is a ceaseless conflict; and, even though the Lord Jesus Christ won the war at Calvary, we must still fight the everyday battles of temptation to sin. Our prayer daily should be, "God deliver us from the multitude of temptations trying to cause us to quit on you. Help us daily to fight any, and all, of Your enemies whenever and wherever we find them."

There are three enemies that are the most determined, skilled, and uncompromising warriors in all of God's creation. They surround us, and are in us, twenty-four hours a day, seven days a week. They are the World, the Devil, and the Flesh, of which none can escape. They all must be fought with the same determination to destroy their influences as they have to destroy us. Let us take a brief look at all three, but I want to focus my primary attention on the last one.

1. The World.

I realize when Christians use that term they mean the influence of not only the natural, physical world, but of the philosophical systems that drive the human race. But I will use the term strictly to speak of the natural world, and will cover the other things under a different term. The World charms us with its beauty, scenery, natural wonders and pleasures. To me, there is nothing more grand, majestic, and beautiful than the mountains. They are places that have always held a great appeal to me; the peace, majesty, and calmness is a balm to my soul. How many hours have I spent alone with God walking in the mountains; and the only time my heart is disappointed is when I have to head back into the town, and get around the noise, hustle, and multitudes once again. I must admit, that one of my great temptations in life is to buy a house in a secluded mountain area, put a fence around it so that I have complete privacy, and just enjoy nature and let the world hurry on without me as it heads to the bottomless pit. I know that isn't a Christian attitude; but that is the call of the mountains to me. It is a danger in my life; and I thank God He has never given me the means to accomplish it. My old Adamic nature is just like a little kid that wants what he wants and doesn't care about the final results. I want, I want, I want! Thank God for a loving Father that gives us what *He* deems best, and not always what we want. In 1 Kings 3:7 King Solomon, the wisest man that ever lived outside of Jesus Christ, called himself *a little child not knowing how to go out or come in*. How much more are we who don't have that special gift of wisdom that was given to him. How thankful I am that my Father knows, and gives me, only what is best.

And then, many times we see the opposite side of the coin, and find that the people living in the mountains are drawn to the sea. On the same note, if they live by the sea, they are drawn sometimes to the deserts. The allurement of travel to foreign lands and strange places entices us to leave our homes, sometimes our families, and many times the will of God. In my own life I live in the high desert of Idaho; but my heart is in places of forests and mountains. But God's place for me right now is in the desert, and my flesh fights me about it all the time. The saying of our society is "the grass is greener on the other side." That is the danger of the world. After travelling from north to south, east to west; from Florida to Canada to Washington, and many other places in between; from living on the East Coast, the Gulf Coast, and spending a good bit of time on the West Coast; after living in Germany, and Romania, and visiting the countries in between them, the only grass I've found to be greener is right in the middle of the desert that I dislike so much. The reason is because it is God's chosen place for me. The grass is only greener in God's oasis, wherever that may be for you. The world offers no peace no matter where you go. Don't spend your life chasing after something that does not exist. The world has no charm to entice me anymore. My true home is New Jerusalem (Revelation 21:2), and the old saying goes, "there's no place like home." Nothing on earth will ever truly satisfy a person again if they have felt the breezes of that city blow on their soul. Until then, the only place the heart of a true Christian will find rest is in the place of God's will for them. Find that place, and you'll never want to leave again, be it in the inner city, a remote mountain village, the steaming jungles of Southeast Asia, or the desert sands of America or Africa. The place doesn't matter; the company does. If you are in God's company, the *place* is irrelevant. The Apostles Paul and Silas were able to sing while in the stocks in a Roman prison because God was a very real Presence to them, and they knew they were there because of their work for Him. God's grace *is* sufficient anywhere, anytime.

How do you defeat the allurement of the world that is trying to entice you away from God's will?

    1. By knowing what God's will is, and making it your first priority. Search the scriptures, seek

good counsel, look for providential circumstances, and listen for the Holy Spirit speaking to your spirit (Mk 12:30).

2. By praying and asking God for a clear vision of what life is really all about. The majority of people spend their entire lives striving to gain a life that has no lasting benefit to themselves or others. For most people, life is a trivial pursuit. Only what's done for Christ will last for eternity; why spend your life following anything else? Yes, you have to make a living for you and your family. However, never make that your primary goal in life, or life will grab hold of you and never let go (2 Tim 2:4).

3. By setting priorities and never allowing anything to usurp their place (Heb 12:1). Here is a good set of priorities to follow: use the acrostic J.O.Y.
   - **J**esus first.
   - **O**thers next.
   - **Y**ourself last.

The Lord Jesus Christ always followed that pattern. A brief look at Calvary is sufficient evidence:
   - *"...thine (will) be done...."* God first.
   - *"to seek and to save that which was lost."* Others next.
   - *"...not my will...."* Himself last.

Nothing that the world had to offer was of any interest to the Lord. He knew it would all be His when He returns anyway. It is the same situation for all of us (1 Pet 1:4).

101

2. *The Devil.*

The sworn enemy of all righteousness, goodness, holiness, and of God and His people.

Re 12:12 "...Woe to the inhabiters of the earth and of the sea! for the devil is come down unto you, having great wrath, because he knoweth that he hath but a short time."

And just how great an enemy is he? Is he really as terrible as he is made out to be? So many people today perceive him to be no threat, or even someone to be desired. How much of today's music openly worships him. Look almost anywhere and you will see some kind of representation of him, even among those who profess to be children of God. If you are in the cyber world, run a Google search with the words "The Occult," and you will be amazed how many web sites there are. I did that this morning and retrieved a list of about fifty-one million sites! Seems like the people interested in the occult are more than just a few.

Just last week while in Portland for more Hep-C treatment, a man parked his motor home next to my camper. He was a motorcycle drag racer, and on his motorcycle trailer were all kinds of sponsors' stickers. At least half of them were skulls or some evil representation of the Devil. When I witnessed to him he claimed to have received Jesus Christ as his Savior! *If* he is saved, what would make him think that promoting evil instead of holiness was the right thing to do? He had one small sticker with a picture of a cross on it, and something written about drag racing for Christ. Did he have one word of scripture anywhere? Of course not. Was there one word about the glory of God or being saved? Not a chance. The man is either totally deceived or lost, but either way, the Devil has him convinced that evil is not something to be avoided, but is to be promoted.

In Acts 16:16-18, we find a woman that was possessed with a spirit of divination. She was a servant of darkness; and yet she followed Paul and Silas declaring to people that they were servants of the most high God and were showing people the way of salvation. It was the evil spirit in her causing her to do that. Why? The evil spirits were trying to get themselves connected with righteousness so that people would be deceived about their true purpose and come to them. Fortunately, Paul had enough spiritual discernment to know what was going on, and he rebuked the evil spirit and commanded it to come out of the woman. Paul didn't want evil promoting good. Today we see young people and adults constantly flashing the "hook'em horns" sign. You've seen it: thumb and pinky extended and the three fingers in between them folded down. It is a sign started by the Satanists which represents the two horns of the Devil upright and the three members of the Trinity put down.

Is he really that bad? Revelation 2:24 speaks of the "depths of Satan," something which no human being, however evil in their doings, has yet to fathom.

Solomon, the wisest man that ever lived wrote briefly of it, and yet he could never know the fullness of the evil that was yet to come.

The Fight For Light

Ec 4:1 "So I returned, and considered all the oppressions that are done under the sun: and behold the tears of such as were oppressed, and they had no comforter; and on the side of their oppressors there was power; but they had no comforter."

In my ministry to the prisons, I hear stories, and read the rap sheets of some of the inmates; such things that will turn a man's stomach. The brutality, lack of fear, and pure vileness is beyond comprehension, and getting worse by the minute. One thing in particular is the vileness done to children these days, even children as young as a few months. This is a sin so vile, and apparently fairly new to our society, that it isn't even mentioned in the Bible. Where do ideas of this kind of degradation come from? Can it be just a twisted mind, or a bad home life? Is it the result of some awful things that have been perpetrated on someone at some time in his life? That's what the psychologists and psychiatrists would have us think. But is it really that, or is it something far worse? Is it a mind that is influenced by the enemy of God and man alike? "The depths of Satan." A being so twisted by envy and jealousy because he was not able to steal the throne and position of God (Isaiah 14:12-14), that he has turned against, and hates with a passion, God and all He stands for. We live in the time just prior to the revealing and work of the "Man of Sin": the Anti-Christ. What is he against? That's simple to figure out: just look at everything God, Jesus Christ, and the Holy Ghost are for, and reverse it. He is *Anti*-Christ.

Look at our world from a truthful perspective. We now have males (I will not call them "men") that look and act like females and vice versa. We now have a complete role reversal in many people's lives. How many times have I seen something walking down the street of whom I could not tell the gender? It is a common occurrence. What is in the mind of these people that don't want to look like what they are? They have the spirit of the Anti-Christ because they do not want to be what God made them to be. Of course they don't consciously think that way. The Devil has given them some plausible reason in their mind to do what they are doing, but He is the one behind it all. And what does God say about it?

De 22:5 "The woman shall not wear that which pertaineth unto a man, neither shall a man put on a woman's garment: for all that do so are abomination unto the LORD thy God."

A male is to look and act like a male, not an effeminate sissy. And one look at Proverbs 31:10-31 will show you how far from God's plan today's women have digressed.

Today it is a common sight to see a woman with her hair cut like a man's military hair cut, and men walking around with ponytails and hair to their waist, sporting a diamond earring! This is all accepted as normal? Some of you right now are thinking that I am just bigoted, and narrow-minded. To that I have to plead guilty, but if you are going to attack my position, then you must realize that you are also attacking God's position and that you are doing the work of Satan. What does God say about long hair on a man and short hair on a woman - 1 Corinthians 11:14-15. Bigoted or holy? It's your call.

105

What about the proliferation of people with tattoos today? What does God say about that subject?

Le 19:28 "Ye shall not make any cuttings in your flesh for the dead, nor print any marks upon you: I am the LORD."

But that sin is becoming more and more prolific all the time, even among women! God makes a beautiful creature, but the Devil wants to destroy her beauty with ugly ink and pictures. And many times, we even see Christians breaking this commandment after they are saved! Their minds have been influenced by the World and the Devil and they don't realize it because they don't spend time with God or reading the Bible. God is not our enemy, the Devil is!

Please allow me to digress from the main focus of this book for a moment and speak as to the condition of our world in general. Who but someone with a mind influenced by this same evil could even remotely think that this world is getting better! Just today I saw an article in Fox News stating that a man wrote a book thanking the Liberals for Saving America. America saved? In what way is America saved? Is anyone really insane enough to believe that America is better now than it was 200 years ago? Haven't we have all read the newspapers and listened to the broadcasts describing what is going on in the world? Getting better? Progress? The only progress this world is making is toward the Bottomless Pit. Don't accuse me of being anti-American. I am most likely more of a patriot than you are; but I am not deceived about America's condition. We read all the time now of home Bible studies being outlawed, prayer and Bibles banned in public schools, and even talk in the government about removing the phrase "in God we trust" from our money. We can't have the Ten Commandments hanging on the walls of public buildings, but Muslim Shari'ah Law is being considered for implementation in our Judicial System.

And what are some of those laws? The following examples are from an article in "Free Thinking" magazine.

1. Islam allows husbands to hit their wives. The Quran says:

"If you fear highhandedness from your wives, remind them of the teaching of God, then ignore them when you go to bed, then hit them." Quran 4:34.

2. Islam commands that robbers should be crucified or mutilated. In 2003, Scotsman Sandy Mitchell faced crucifixion in Saudi Arabia. He was beaten and tortured until he confessed a crime he did not commit. Quran 5:33

3. Islam orders death for Muslim and possible death for non-Muslim critics of Muhammad and the Quran. This law was put into effect in England in 2007, and can be found in "Reliance of the Traveler" pp 597-598, 8.07.

4. Islam orders the death of apostates (anyone not a Muslim) – Sura 9:11-12. That is the complete opposite of the Bible:

This is only a small part, but it makes my point. This is the law America wants over the Ten Commandments of a Holy God? This is what America's liberal thinkers call progress? It certainly is progress, but all in the wrong direction.

And what does the Bible say about all this?

2Co 11:4 *"For if he that cometh preacheth another Jesus, whom we have not preached, or if ye receive another spirit, which ye have not received, or another gospel, which ye have not accepted, ye might well bear with him."*

Mt 7:13-14 *"Enter ye in at the strait gate: for wide is the gate, and broad is the way, that leadeth to destruction, and many there be which go in thereat: Because strait is the gate, and narrow is the way, which leadeth unto life, and few there be that find it."*

Please understand something at this point. It is not my intention to sermonize, and I'm not saying that most people are doing the things mentioned above because they are against God and His ways. They simply do it because of peer pressure or the idea that it isn't hurting anyone, or that it is just something they want to do. My purpose in bringing these things out is to show that God's way is far different from the way most people realize it is. Many Christians go through life thinking their lives are pleasing to God, when in reality they don't know what *is* pleasing to Him. So many people fit into the category of the following verse:

Jud 17:6 *"In those days there was no king in Israel, but every man did that which was right in his own eyes."*

We live in the days of situation ethics and pragmatism: In other words – if it feels good, do it. Most people have no "king," just like Israel in the verse, and so they are their own king and judge of what is right. That thinking is what has led us to the current state of affairs in our world. What is the world's problem? Here it is in a nutshell:

Jer 6:16 *"Thus saith the LORD, Stand ye in the ways, and see, and ask for the old paths, where is the good way, and walk therein, and ye shall find rest for your souls. But they said, We will not walk therein."*

How do you combat the Devil's influence in your life? The best way is to get as far away from his outlets of poison as possible. The liberal news media; TV, movies, and music that promote immorality and wickedness; pornography in all forms; and public educational systems are good places to start. If you need to, put a "parental lock" on your Internet to keep your children, and YOU (by using a random password that not even you know) away from detrimental web sites. Make a start with those and you'll be well on your way to curbing the Devil's influence in your life. As an illustration please consider this: a 2011 study by divorce court judges in England showed that in one-third of divorces, FaceBook was a contributing factor. That is a reality that happened in my own extended family!

But since many of us realize the degradation of the world because of Satan's influence, I will not dwell on this point any longer. I wish to focus our attention on the biggest fight, and the greatest enemy of all true followers of Christ in this life.

3. The "Self Life." (The flesh).

The greatest battleground in the Fight for Light is always within our own selves. The Apostle Paul puts it well when describing his own spiritual battle:

Ro 7:14-21 "For we know that the law is spiritual: but I am carnal, sold under sin. For that which I do I allow not: for what I would, that do I not; but what I hate, that do I. If then I do that which I would not, I consent unto the law that it is good. Now then it is no more I that do it, but sin that dwelleth in me. For I know that in me (that is, in my flesh,) dwelleth no good thing: for to will is present with me; but how to perform that which is good I find not. For the good that I would I do not: but the evil which I would not, that I do. Now if I do that I would not, it is no more I that do it, but sin that dwelleth in me. I find then a law, that, when I would do good, evil is present with me."

And again:
<u>*Ga 5:17*</u> *"For the flesh lusteth against the Spirit, and the Spirit against the flesh: and these are contrary the one to the other: so that ye cannot do the things that ye would."*

Was Paul a fool to think and write such things, or did he have a revelation of our true nature that many have not yet seen.

Our culture says that man is basically a good creation with a few flaws. The Bible says that man is totally corrupt from the cradle to the grave, with no redeeming qualities of his own. Notice the verse says the flesh and Spirit are contrary to each other. What that translates to in our daily lives is nothing less than unrelenting war on our own flesh. According to James 1:17, anything good we have in us came from God. If an unregenerate person (someone not saved) has some good qualities in him or her, they still received those qualities from God.

> Jas 1:17 "Every good gift and every perfect gift is from above, and cometh down from the Father of lights, with whom is no variableness, neither shadow of turning."

Therein lies the reason man needs a supernatural Saviour; something I will cover in a later chapter. Man's nature is basically corrupt, and that applies to both the regenerated and unregenerated as well. Even our natural desires in daily life are corrupt when you really think about it. Let me give just a few examples:

Which would most of us rather eat, spinach or ice cream? Ice cream of course. But which one is better for our physical well being?

Which would most of us rather do - play, rest and relax, or work? Certainly not work. The saying is: A bad day fishing is better than a good day at work.

Or: I owe, I owe, so it's off to work I go. One man said this: I have never liked working. To me a job is an invasion of privacy.

Why do humans invent such sayings? Because deep down, even the most optimistic have to agree that the flesh is corrupt.

Why do we have a 50-75% divorce rate even here in the United States? People are not satisfied with what they have. They are not willing to work through their problems and fix what is wrong with themselves. The spouse is always to blame for everything. The grass is greener with someone else. They have a microwave mentality: fix it quick or forget it. My wife and I make up a small percentage of society these days. We met in high school and have been together ever since; forty-one years as of this writing. Have there been temptations along the way? Of course there have, for both of us. But we took a vow in the sight of God to love and stay with each other "for better or worse, in sickness and in health, till death do us part," NOT until we get tired of each other and someone else looks more promising. We have had to fight our own corrupt natures just like everyone else. It's called character; something that is definitely on the wane in our world today.

The self-nature of man is incorrigible. That is why the Lord Jesus Christ tells us to pick up our cross and follow Him; He knows that although His way is not easy sometimes, it is a far better choice to follow Him rather than ourselves. The Apostle Paul tells us the same thing, but in a different context. Paul certainly had his share of outward crosses to carry, but I believe what he is teaching here is something deeper. Outward problems such as health, financial, or family problems, are certainly all crosses that we must carry from time to time. But I believe the greater meaning is the cross we must pick up and die on everyday, the cross of the Crucified Life. We must put to death the the old nature. Death to the old ruler and sovereign of our life, and begin a new life lived to the One that created that life.

This battle with self is a result of two things: 1. our own flesh not liking the circumstances, and 2. the Devil driving or causing problems. Once again, it is a fight of the mind. Physical problems can, and are, many times relieved by the drugs available to us. I realize that the drugs can also make you feel terrible, like Morphine and Dilaudid do to me. I'm not discounting that fact. However, I think all of us would rather put up with a sick stomach because of side effects of those drugs instead of the intense pain we would suffer without them. The biggest fight for me is simply that I get sick and tired of being sick and tired. And unless you want to start taking even more drugs like anti-depressants (which I've done) or Valium so that you forget about life entirely, you will find yourself in a relentless struggle. What is the choice of most people? Give me the drugs! No, this is a spiritual battle of the first order. It can make or break your newly found relationship with God, and all the lessons you have learned along your journey.

LOSE THE BATTLE WITH SELF, AND YOU LOSE THEM ALL! What do victories of any kind amount to if the spiritual battle with self, (to become what the Lord wants you to become), is lost? In speaking of spiritual warfare, the Lord Jesus Christ writes the following:

113

Mr 8:36 "For what shall it profit a man, if he shall gain the whole world, and lose his own soul?"

My subject in this chapter is not about our souls, but our lives after our souls are secure in Him. However, if a person loses their soul because of not accepting the Lord as their Savior, they have lost the first, and most important, battle with self. This topic illustrates the fact that the spiritual warfare in our lives far outweighs any other battles we will face.

What is the battle ground?

Very simply it is this: who is on the throne of your life - God or you?

Who decides what you will do in any particular situation?

Who decides your career choice? Who decides the person you will marry? Who decides where you attend church; where you will live; how you will spend your money; what you watch and listen to; who your friends will be; what your life will be; etc.?

Is God living His life through you or are you living your life according to your own passions and ideas? That is the great battle ground of the Christian life.

Some of you are probably thinking right now that I've really gone over the edge and have started meddling in things that are none of my business.

Have I, or am I just giving you today's examples of Christ in the garden when He said "not my will, but Thine be done." What more proof of what God wants do we need than that; the Son of God Himself surrendering to His Father's will. Who was on the throne of Jesus's life? Was it His own human nature, or did God have complete control of the life of Jesus Christ? You know the answer to that.

Jn 8:29 "And he that sent me is with me: the Father hath not left me alone; for I do always those things that please him."

Would to God that we can someday have that testimony ourselves! "I do always those things that please Him." Christ on earth was the living example of Revelation 4:11 that we discussed when talking of God's Sovereignty. Jesus Christ never thought, spoke, or acted in any way with which God was not pleased. Oh God, if I could just live two days in a row like that. And the truth is, if we will fight to die daily to ourselves, we can live that kind of a life. Certainly we can not live surrendered 100% of the time because we are too corrupt and sinful for that to happen. However, we can live above sin far more than most of us do. Would that not be the greatest battle to lose in life? To lose to yourself and let God have the victory over your complete being?

Oswald Chambers put it this way:

"No one experiences complete sanctification without going through a "white funeral" - the burial of the old life. If there has never been this crucial moment of change through death, sanctification will never be more than an elusive dream. There must be a "white funeral;" a death with only one resurrection-a resurrection into the life of Jesus Christ. Nothing can defeat a life like

115

this. It has oneness with God for only one purpose-to be a witness for Him."

A.W. Tozer puts it another way:
Our woes began when God was forced out of His central shrine and "things" were allowed to enter. Within the human heart "things" have taken over. Men have now by nature no peace within their hearts, for God is crowned there no longer, but there in the moral dusk stubborn and aggressive usurpers fight among themselves for first place on the throne."[6]

Where is the battle ground?

The answer to that question is many times not an easy one to believe or accept. For many, it is the ground of suffering. The purpose of God allowing, or even directing, our path in the way of suffering, is so that we see how frail we are and how great God is. Many times it is also for the purpose of getting us where He wants us to be in life. When we begin to see that, it makes us more willing to die to self. And the further into that revelation we go, the more willing we are to die to our self-life.

In his biography, Robert Murray M'Cheyne, saw the absolute need for affliction as a child of God. Speaking particularily of the ministerial aspect he said this:
"I hope this affliction will be blessed to me. I always feel much need of God's afflicting hand. In

---

[6] A. W. Tozer, *The Pursuit of God,* (Christian Publications Inc., Harrisburg, PA, 1948, Kindle Edition), p. 184.

the whirl of active labor there is so little time for watching, and for bewailing, and seeking grace to oppose the sins of our ministry, that I always feel it a blessed thing when the Saviour takes me aside from the crowd, as He took the blind man out of the town, and removes the veil, and clears away obscuring mists, and by his word and Spirit leads to deeper peace and a holier walk."[7]

God is clear in His instructions to us about the character He wishes us to have:

Ro 8:29 "For whom he did foreknow, he also did predestinate to be conformed to the image of his Son, that he might be the firstborn among many brethren."

If you have spent time in the Bible then you know what that image is. It is found in Isaiah 53:

Isa 53:3 "He is despised and rejected of men; a man of sorrows, and acquainted with grief: and we hid as it were our faces from him; he was despised, and we esteemed him not."

A.W. Tozer said:

"Self is the opaque veil that hides the Face of God from us. It can be removed only in spiritual experience, never by mere instruction. As well try to instruct leprosy out of our system. There must

---

[7] Ibid, Location 1514.

be a work of God in destruction before we are free. We must *invite* the cross to do its deadly work within us. We must bring our self-sins to the cross for judgment. We must prepare ourselves for an ordeal of suffering in some measure like that through which our Saviour passed when He suffered under Pontius Pilate."[8] (Italics mine).

The pathway to having real fellowship and fruitfulness, and of living a life pleasing to the One who created us, is a two-fold path: 1. getting to see ourselves as God sees us, and 2. us seeing God as He is. In our lives, as twenty-first century beings, those two paths are very rarely talked about, and, even more sadly, rarely ever preached about in today's pulpits. Quite the opposite is true. Today the philosophy is Epicureanism: eat, drink, and be merry. Comfort is the order of the day. And much of what is called Christianity today is exactly the same. The Prosperity Gospel is preached constantly, especially by charismatic TV ministers. You've heard it – Give your life (and especially your money) to God (and me), and you'll be healthy, wealthy, and wise. The "give to get" mentality is everywhere in today's pulpits. "Just plant your seed faith by sending us five-hundred dollars." The "give to please" philosophy is unheard of.

Why did Jesus Christ give His life willingly? Was it to gain something for Himself, or was it simply to give to God the best Christ had to give. Yes, He knew He would be glorified, and would be purchasing a wife for Himself (the Bride of Christ), but His primary motive was, once again, "not my will." His glory and Bride were secondary

8

to His primary motive. It pleased His Father, and purchased eternal redemption for "whosoever will." What was the cost? A perfect home in Heaven, that He left for thirty-three years, and of living a life without the creature comforts that you and I take so much for granted. And, after all that, a ministry of being rejected by those He loved and helped most. Subsequently he died a torturous, horrible death on the cross. That was the price of victory!

And what is God's plan for you and me?

1Pe 5:8-11 *"Be sober, be vigilant; because your adversary the devil, as a roaring lion, walketh about, seeking whom he may devour: Whom resist stedfast in the faith, knowing that the same afflictions are accomplished in your brethren that are in the world. But the God of all grace, who hath called us unto his eternal glory by Christ Jesus, after that ye have suffered a while, make you perfect, stablish, strengthen, settle you. To him be glory and dominion for ever and ever. Amen."*

The entire purpose of suffering is to make us see how frail, sinful, and needy of God we are. But it is a fight, literally, to the death of the old nature. Allow me to quote A.W. Tozer once again:

"Let us examine our burden. It is altogether an interior one. It attacks the heart and the mind and reaches the body only from within. First, there is the burden of pride. The labor of self-love is a heavy one indeed. Think for yourself whether much of your sorrow has not arisen from someone speaking slightingly of you. As long as you set yourself up as a little god to which you must be loyal there will be those who will delight to offer affront to your idol. How then can you hope to have inward peace? The heart's fierce effort to protect itself from every slight, to shield its touchy honor from the bad opinion of friend and enemy, will never let the mind have rest. Continue this fight through the years and the burden will become intolerable. Yet the sons of earth are carrying this burden continually, challenging every word spoken against them, cringing under every criticism, smarting under each fancied slight, tossing sleepless if another is preferred before them. Such a burden as this is not necessary to bear. Jesus calls us to His rest, and meekness is His method. The meek man cares not at all who is greater than he, for he has long ago decided that the esteem of the world is not worth the effort. He develops toward himself a kindly sense of humor and learns to say, "Oh, so you have been overlooked? They have placed someone else before you? They have whispered that you are pretty small stuff after all? And now you feel hurt because the world is saying about you the very things you have been saying about yourself? Only yesterday you were telling God that you were nothing, a mere worm of the dust. Where is your consistency? Come on, humble yourself, and cease to care what men think." The meek man is not a human mouse afflicted with a sense of his own inferiority. Rather he may be in his moral life as bold as a lion and as strong as Samson; but he has stopped being fooled about himself. He has accepted God's estimate of his own life. He knows he is as weak and helpless as God has declared him to be, but paradoxically, he knows at the same time that he is in the sight of God of more importance than angels. *In himself, nothing; in God, everything. That is his motto.*" (italics mine)[9]

I recently purchased a DVD which gave the stories of many of the Medal of Honor recipients from the time of the Civil War through Afghanistan. The men are honored because they gave their lives in order to save the lives of others around them. And they are made out to be heroes because of their loyalty to their comrades. I'm not trying to take one thing away from those men; they most certainly are heroes. But in reality, most of them did what they did because of training, spur of the moment thinking, and adrenalin. It was not a conscious thought when they woke up in the morning that they were going to look for a way to die that day so others could live. Perhaps, for some of them, at the moment of decision there was the thought of sacrificing for others, but again, they certainly did not go looking for a way to die in order to be a hero and help their buddies.

But for those Christians who are trying to live the crucified life, struggling to die to the self-life is what we are faced with everyday. It is something we choose. We must make a conscious effort all day long to be aware of ourselves dethroning God in our lives and enthroning ourselves. We must die to our entire old nature in order

IBID, p. 79.

for God to live His fullest through us. Most mornings I pray before getting out of bed. I usually tell God: so far we're doing good, Lord, but in a minute I have to get out of bed and then the struggle begins. (Actually just getting out of bed is the first struggle.) But I ask God to get on the throne first thing, and help me not to kick Him off it at any time that day. I must admit, I want to be the recipient of God's Medal of Honor. He has some crowns that He wants to bestow on us for our faithful love and work for Him. I want that crown! He gives it to us for our glory in Heaven, and for His glory as we cast it at His feet because we know that we could never accomplish the sacrifice on our own. The only way to win those crowns is the self-crucified life.

Some of you are right now thinking that this is not a way of life that you really want to experience. It can't be worth all that. But please, stay with me, and we will cover the answer to that below.

Is the victory a permanent one?

"The cross is rough, and it is deadly, but it is effective. It does not keep its victim hanging there forever. There comes a moment when its work is finished and the suffering victim dies. After that is resurrection glory and power, and the pain is forgotten for joy that the veil is taken away and we have entered in actual spiritual experience the Presence of the living God." A.W. Tozer.[10]

The self-crucified life seems to be one, which at some point, becomes second nature. We become constantly aware of who and what we are, and who and what God is. We are no longer self-deceived, and we willingly stay as far away from the throne of our lives as possible. Instead of something we do, it becomes something we are. But even at that, the old man is still lurking about in the shadows, and will occasionally usurp the throne. Isaiah said it best:

Isa 64:6 "But we are all as an unclean thing, and all our righteousnesses are as filthy rags; and we all do fade as a leaf; and our iniquities, like the wind, have taken us away."

The blood of the Lord Jesus Christ cleanses us from all sin, but nowhere is it said that sin is removed from our lives. The Apostle Paul knew this only too well. Look at his lamentation of his own life:

Ro 7:14 -25 "For we know that the law is spiritual: but I am carnal, sold under sin. For that which I do I allow not: for what I would, that do I not; but what I hate, that do I. If then I do that which I would not, I consent unto the law that it is good. Now then it is no more I that do it, but sin that dwelleth in me. For I know that in me (that is, in my flesh,)

IBID, p. 36.

dwelleth no good thing: for to will is present with me; but *how to perform that which is good I find not. For the good that I would I do not: but the evil which I would not, that I do. Now if I do that I would not, it is no more I that do it, but sin that dwelleth in me. I find then a law, that, when I would do good, evil is present with me. For I delight in the law of God after the inward man: But I see another law in my members, warring against the law of my mind, and bringing me into captivity to the law of sin which is in my members. O wretched man that I am! who shall deliver me from the body of this death? I thank God through Jesus Christ our Lord. So then with the mind I myself serve the law of God; but with the flesh the law of sin."*

This is his testimony as a saved man. And, once again, that is the reason he tells us that we must die *daily*. It is a never-ending war on the flesh until the day the Lord calls us Home.

Is it worth the fight?

In John 15:1-8 we see a principle: God is never closer to the vine than when He is pruning it. I mentioned previously the crowns that God awards us for living the self-less life. My greatest desire in life is to hear my Lord and God says these words to me:

Mt 25:21 "His lord said unto him, Well done, thou good and faithful servant: thou hast been faithful over a few things, I will make thee ruler over many things: enter thou into the joy of thy lord."

The way of the cross almost seems like a masochistic way of life: willingly accepting and rejoicing in suffering. But allow me to give the testimony of my own experience. After all the pain, sorrow, disappointments, depression, despair, and loss of almost everything in my life, I would not trade these last years for all the prosperity in the world. I know my Lord better than I ever have. I have a closer walk with Him. I have learned many spiritual lessons, and I am more useful to Him now than at any time in the last thirty years of salvation. I am not afraid of the Lord's dealings with me anymore. I know what I am, and I know what He is, and how much He truly loves me. And you have no cause for fear either. If God gives you the privilege of suffering so that He can draw close to you to teach you the love and compassion of God, don't be afraid of it. It is the gift of God.

2Co 12:7-10 "And lest I should be exalted above measure through the abundance of the revelations, there was given to me a thorn in the flesh, the messenger of Satan to buffet me, lest I should be exalted above measure. For this thing I besought the Lord thrice, that it might depart from me. And he said unto me, My grace is sufficient for thee: for my

strength is made perfect in weakness. Most gladly therefore
will I rather glory in my infirmities, that the power of Christ
may rest upon me. Therefore I take pleasure in infirmities, in
reproaches, in necessities, in persecutions, in distresses for
Christ's sake: for when I am weak, then am I strong."

Jn 12:24 "Verily, verily, I say unto you, Except a
corn of wheat fall into the ground and die, it abideth alone:
but if it die, it bringeth forth much fruit."

That is what He is trying to do to all His children; get
us to willingly die to our self life. In other words, die to
being king of your own life, in order for Him to be King
of your life. Allow God to direct every thought, every
word, every deed, every moment, of every day, for the
rest of your life. It is *the way* to real life, peace, and joy.

"There is a sweet word in Exodus (3:7), which
was pointed out to me the other day by a poor
bereaved child of God: *"I know their sorrows."*
Study that; it fills the soul. Another word like it is
in Psalm 103:14: "He knoweth our frame." May
your own soul, and that of your dear friends, be
fed by these things. A dark hour makes Jesus
bright."

Robert Murray M'Cheyne.[11]

---

[11] Andrew A. Bonar, *The Biography of Robert Murray M'Cheyne,*
(Zondervan Publishing House, Grand Rapids, MI, Kindle edition),
Location 1043.

In closing this chapter, please allow me to once again quote the words of A.W. Tozer. The reason I use his, and M'Cheyne's material so much, is that they were men who lived this subject like very few ever have; it was the whole essence of their incredible lives and ministries:

"We sense that the call is for us, but still we fail to draw near, and the years pass and we grow old and tired in the outer courts of the tabernacle. What doth hinder us? The answer usually given, simply that we are "cold," will not explain all the facts. There is something more serious than coldness of heart, something that may be back of that coldness and be the cause of its existence. What is it? What but the presence of a veil in our hearts? A veil not taken away as the first veil was, but which remains there still shutting out the light and hiding the face of God from us. It is the veil of our fleshly fallen nature living on, un-judged within us, un-crucified, and un-repudiated. It is the close-woven veil of the self-life which we have never truly acknowledged, of which we have been secretly ashamed, and which for these reasons we have never brought to the judgment of the cross. It is not too mysterious, this opaque veil, nor is it hard to identify. We have but to look in our own hearts and we shall see it there, sewn and patched and repaired it may be, but there nevertheless, an enemy to our lives and an effective block to our spiritual progress. This veil is not a beautiful thing and it is not a thing about which we commonly care to talk, but I am addressing the thirsting souls who are determined to follow God, and I know they will not turn back because the way leads temporarily through the blackened hills. The urge of God within them will assure their continuing the pursuit. They will face the facts however unpleasant and endure the cross for the joy set before them. So I am bold to name the threads out of which this inner veil is woven. It is woven of the fine threads of the self-life, the hyphenated sins of the human spirit. They are not something we do, they are something we are, and therein lies both their subtlety and their power. To be specific, the self-sins are these: self-righteousness, self-pity, self-confidence, self-sufficiency, self-admiration, self-love and a host of others like them. They dwell too deep within us and are too much a part of our natures to come to our attention till the light of God is focused upon them. The grosser manifestations of these sins, egotism, exhibitionism, self-promotion, are strangely tolerated in Christian leaders even in circles of impeccable orthodoxy. They are so much in evidence as actually, for many people, to become identified with the gospel. I trust it is not a cynical observation to say that they appear these days to be a requisite for popularity in some sections of the Church visible. Promoting self under the guise of promoting Christ is currently so common as to excite little notice."

Brethren, you must fight on! There *is* victory to be won. The test of a person's character is not how many times he gets knocked down. The real test is how many times he gets back up. If you steal the throne of your life away from God a hundred times a day, repent and give it back to Him a hundred times a day. What does it take to keep you down?

One of my earthly heroes is a fighter I will simply refer to as O____ He is from Russia, and I've watched him fight numerous times. I have seen him so beaten up and bloody that he literally could barely see or stand; but there was one thing about him that impressed me more than everything else: He never once gave up in a fight, and never lost by anything other than a knockout. What a testimony of character! How is it, brethren, that lost men can find the character and intestinal fortitude to fight like that, and Christians can't, or won't. He, and other men like him, are examples to me not to let the Devil ever win. If God allows him to knock me out, fine, but throw in the towel? By the grace of God – never. No surrender to the enemies of God!

I recently took a three-day trip to the Sawtooth National Forest, about two hours from my home in Boise, ID. A friend was kind enough to loan me the use of his cabin; so I packed up my fishing gear, far too many books, my laptop, food, etc., etc., and headed off for a few days by myself. Pam and I needed a break from each other since we were getting on each other's nerves after fifteen months of being together everyday, during the worst of my trial. I decided to find a creek I had read about, that was a good bit off the beaten path; so I loaded up my 4x4 pickup and took off. I found the dirt road I was supposed to take and got a half mile off the asphalt road when I found some snow in the road. I put the truck in four-wheel drive and plowed through it; it should not have been a problem. Wrong assumption. I progressed

129

half-way through the seventy-five yard patch and promptly sank the wheels deep in a drift. And what did I have to dig it out with? A tire iron. No shovel, no sand for under the wheels. I was never a Boy Scout (always be prepared). A tire iron and a tree limb. I dug for two hours to no avail. Because of my health condition, I was exhausted after ten minutes of digging. I kept praying for God to help me directly or send someone along. He did neither; so, I kept digging! Every ten minutes I tried to move the truck again; no dice. OK, it was time to call the police in town and see if they could send someone to pull me out. Surprise, there was no cell phone service. Time had come to walk and find someone to help me. Please realize that this is spring in a summer resort area; lots of houses with nobody in them. I finally found someone, and he loaned me a shovel. By this time I was about to fall down from fatigue, and now I had to really start digging. Could I have walked into town and hired a tow truck? Possibly; but I would have been just as tired by the time I got there, and I might not have found one available, and been out a hundred dollars or more if I did find one. So, fight on. Pray on. After roughly twenty minutes of digging with the shovel I was able to move the truck.

The point I'm trying to make is that, even though the Lord delivered me to get out of there, the task of digging that truck out would have been much easier two years ago when I was still healthy. I would have been an inconvenience, but not a battle. EASE IS NOT THE ISSUE. The issue is, will you fight on?

In the elite corps of the military, ease is not any concern at all, but the mission is all-important. And those corps know that the way to build an elite, tough, determined, non-quitter is to persecute him. Push him to the breaking point and beyond. He will either quit, or quit quitting! But for us, there is no cause to quit because God has promised us a power far beyond our own. We read it earlier in Paul's testimony: "My grace is sufficient for thee." Is God's grace sufficient? You will learn that it is, or you will quit on God.

Ro 8:18 "For I reckon that the sufferings of this present time are not worthy to be compared with the glory which shall be revealed in us."

Job 24:13 "They are of those that rebel against the light; they know not the ways thereof, nor abide in the paths thereof."

Chapter Eleven: Treatment

When discussing the subject of treatment, I certainly will not be intruding into the areas of medical science, a field I realize is out of my area of expertise, even though I have dealt with that profession every day for the last few years. In reality, I know a great deal about my condition. I've even had to correct some nurses and physicians assistants from time to time that tried to add to, or change, what my doctors and I knew to be right. I've had some doctors and nurses surprised at how much I do know about my case. I think it is a good idea to be as informed as possible about any area affecting my life. However, I would never interfere with the treatment plan my regular doctors have prescribed; I certainly do not know all that they know, nor do I have their experience. No, in this chapter I will deal only with that of which I am certain.

The treatment I want to deal with is the healing treatment of the soldier in this "Fight For Light." A battle that can drag on for many years and sometimes decades. A battle that eventually wearies the body, soul, and spirit of even the strongest Christian. One of the questions I posed at the beginning of this book was: are you sick and tired of being sick and tired? Are you just worn out fighting the battle even when you realize it is a battle sent from God to mold and make you into something beautiful and useful for Him? Do you get tired even of what God wants after awhile? I certainly have become tired, and not just of His will, but even of Him! Even to the point of telling Him I would rather have died in the hospital than to fight this protracted battle. You may say, what an unspiritual attitude! Yes it is, isn't it. So be it.

Lay all the charges at my feet that you like, but please do not judge me too harshly until you have walked in my shoes. By the grace of God I will have the charity to do the same for you. The fact is, I don't know of one person who has fought a long term chronic illness that has *not* reached that point.

I have a dear friend that I will simply call S___ He and his wonderful wife have both been long term soldiers of the cross, and have done much for the cause of Christ and His Saints. Both have fought serious, long term, physical battles. S___ has even written books of his own on the subject of Christian suffering. But in talking with him privately not long ago he also spoke about being tired of being tired, and sick of being sick. He was just plain weary of fighting. And I know other great men of God, whose names I will not mention here, who have been in the same situation. So too, the strongest of the strong get worn down eventually by the constant pain in the body, and the constant warfare with the world, the flesh, and the Devil. Even as a hard rock will eventually be worn down by the constant drip of running water.

Allow me to quote the medical profession in their treatment of Combat Fatigue in Vietnam:

"There is an end point in the available resources of any individual. There is a place in time when all the positive motivation, training, and leadership are not enough, when the soldier's capability and willingness to continue begin to deteriorate. If there is no chance of relief or *no additional factors to sustain him*, the potentiality for combat exhaustion exists. It is also important to note that this energy juncture may begin to

134

indicate his impairment as a solider in spite of his physical presence. His judgment is not as good, alertness may suffer, and his willingness to take chances may disappear. He and his men may become physical casualties long before they become psychological casualties."[12] [italics mine]

I read somewhere, years ago, of Ho Chi Minh, the leader of the Communist forces in North Vietnam saying about the war, that, even though they were outnumbered and outgunned, they would still win the war. He said, "All we have to do is not lose; the Americans will eventually get tired of chasing us through the jungles and will go home." He was right.

Brethren, the enemy we face never tires of the battle. The Devil never stops fighting our heart, mind, and spirit in his attempt to get us to quit. And when people give in to his pressure and leave the battle front, many times they never return, but simply quit on God and His plan for their lives. That is exactly why the Devil keeps the pressure on. He knows eventually many Christians will either quit on God entirely, or will quit on His perfect will for their lives and become mediocre Christians. Our churches are filled with them. Do they have to quit? Have they been given more to deal with than God can get them through? No, of course not. But our hearts and minds are great deceivers, and the constant whisperings of the Devil in our ears often forces us to believe that we can go no further. It is not true.

---

[12] Ronald J. Glasser M.D., *365 Days,* (George Braziller, Inc., New York, New York 10016, 1971), p. 175.

So what is the cure? The book quoted above, I believe is the definitive work on the war in Vietnam. If you really want to know what went through the mind of the average soldier, the book was written by Ronald J. Glasser M.D., who was a doctor at Zama Army Hospital in Japan at the time. That hospital treated thousands of soldiers wounded in the war. In the chapter called "Gentlemen It Works," they discussed the treatment of Combat Fatigue, and found out that the best treatment for it was to temporarily remove a soldier from the combat, but to keep him close enough to the war zone where he could still feel as if he belonged. His unit identity was not taken away from him, and the emphasis of the doctors was getting him back to normal and back to work, rather than focusing on the problem. They found that focusing on the psychological problem of combat fatigue only served to make a soldier a permanent psychological casualty. The soldiers were never allowed to think they would be going home, but that they would be going back to their units and the war. The doctors found out, after treating many cases, that those sent to rear R&R areas to recuperate, far away from the war, many times became permanent psychological casualties. They would not return to the war. There was nothing *physically* wrong with them; it was all in the way they perceived the situation in their minds.[13]

In my own situation, when I had to return to Portland the second time for another round of treatment, the physical battle was easier than it was the first time. I didn't have to under go a transplant this time, and my body responded to the medications better than the first.

---

[13] Ibid, p. 149-178.

But the spiritual battle was much more intense; I just didn't want to do it. I was tired of the whole thing. I was sick of doctors and nurses, needles, blood tests, hospitals, questions, the poking and prodding, and especially Portland, Oregon. I apologize to anyone reading this that is a Portland native or resident; but I have to say that I absolutely hate the place. I've seen many cars and buildings there that have a sign or bumper sticker saying "Keep Portland Weird." And that's what the place is; it is one of the most spiritually dark places I've ever been in. I don't like weird. My spirit doesn't like weird. And my God doesn't like weird. So all these things combined added up to a very large spiritual battle for me. All I wanted to do was quit and go home, even to the point sometimes of not caring if the treatment failed as a result. And what would that have accomplished? It would have put me out of the will of God, hurt His reputation in the eyes of some people, and eventually caused me to lose my life.

What was the answer to this problem? Put the helmet back on, strap on the gear, and head deeper into the battle than ever before. The answer was to do exactly the opposite of what I was being tempted to do. I had to fight my way into a deeper relationship with God, because I knew that He was my only salvation. John the Baptist said it best, *"He must increase, but I must decrease,"* John 3:30. I knew I did not have the strength and ability to fight such an enemy, and indeed, that is exactly what God wanted to show me. I've heard the verse often quoted but little understood:

Jn 15:5 "J am the vine, ye are the branches: He that abideth in me, and J in him, the same bringeth forth much fruit: for without me ye can do nothing."

My reliance on "self" had to be broken, before my reliance on Jesus Christ could be complete. I was deceived about my own spirituality and closeness to God, just as many Christians are. After thirty years of salvation, I thought I had a good understanding of my condition and relationship with the Lord. Oh boy, did I have a lot to learn (and still do). God's greatness had to be revealed in a way I had never seen before, before I could realize my own true weakness and spiritual condition. And the only way to experience His revelation was to get closer to Him. The problem with that is two-fold.

First: The closer you get to God, the closer you get to the Devil. When you decide to go deep with God, you are going to run into the Devil like never before. The reason is that the closer you are to God, the bigger threat you are to the Devil's kingdom.

Second: Deuteronomy 4:24 and Hebrews 12:29 say that God is a consuming fire. Look at any flame, large or small, and tell me where the hottest and purest part of the flame is. If you say it is in the center, in the dark blue flame, and not in the larger yellow flame further from the center, you are correct. There is no fancy dancing yellow flame, no show to be seen; it is quiet and subdued. So if you are going to get to God, in the center, you are going to pass through a lot of flame, and it will get hotter and hotter as you approach the center. But that is the dwelling place of God. As you go deeper toward God, more and more of the dross of your own life burns off, you become purer and purer, and you begin to see Him as never before. But when you get to the center, you find yourself in the place of the three Hebrew men in the book of Daniel. When they were cast into the fire, a fourth man was in there with them, the Son of God. The flame, heat, and smoke had no effect on them.

When you begin to get close to the center, and take a good look at yourself, you will be amazed at the transformation that has taken place in your life. What happened to all those things that used to be so important to you? If they were important to God they are still part of you. If they weren't important to Him, the fire has removed the importance of them to you also. Just as Paul said when he spoke of enduring the loss of all things and counting them as dung. But oh the joy of the purity of it all. "Self" being revealed and destroyed, and God being revealed and exalted. And a new dedication, determination, and love that drives us to serve Him as HE desires. Thoughts of quitting now begin to fade and return to us far less frequently. And they are fairly easily put down in our minds because of the joy of the new fellowship with, and love for, our Lord and master.

The treatment, as I've said before, is "no surrender to the enemies of God." Make a determination in your life to quit quitting. Put to the Cross of the Lord Jesus Christ every thought of giving up, and watch the Lord do new things in you to draw you closer to Him.

Listen to some of the words of the grand old hymn "Am I A Soldier Of The Cross":

Are there no foes for me to face? Must I not stem the flood?

Is this vile world a friend to grace, to help me on to God?

Sure I must fight if I would reign, increase my courage, Lord!
I'll bear the toil, endure the pain, supported by Thy Word.

Isaac Watts, Thomas A. Arne

Here are just a few practical suggestions for you to use as part of your daily armor. This is my own personal list I try my best to use everyday:

1. Rejoice evermore. Pray without ceasing. In every thing give thanks... – 1 Thessalonians 5:16.
2. Sing the songs of Zion. My wife and I try to sing something from the hymn book every evening – Psalm 104:33.
3. Get off the throne of your life. Pray for the grace to accomplish it – Luke 9:23.
4. Finish the race. Finish clean. Finish with joy – 2 Timothy 4:7.
5. Be content – Philippians 4:11.
6. Keep a merry heart - Proverbs 15:15.
7. Think on things that are pure, lovely, and of good report – Philippians 4:8.
8. Never miss a day of reading the word of God and prayer – Psalm 119:28.

Chapter Twelve: Death Can Be A Gift

We have talked much about the death of the "self-life" in the Fight For Light, and I think I have shown the absolute benefits of living that life. But what about physical death?

In my ministry to the chronically ill, I visited a dear lady I will call L____. She suffers from kidney failure, has had two transplants already, and is in need of a third. Due to some other complications she is not even being considered for one. She sits at home unable to do much of anything. When I sat down with her, she started to cry and asked me, "Why won't God just take me home?" The answer to that is simple (although it may seem trite), but it is certainly not an easy one to accept. The reason? God still has something for you to do! And just what is that? To that question I cannot possibly have an answer; that is for God to reveal. But go back to what I said in chapter six about Job. There was only one thing he could do, but he didn't do it.

However, allow me to relate a true story I once heard about a quadriplegic Christian woman named Annie. Annie could do nothing for herself, but she still wanted to do something for the Lord she loved. Her family set her up with an automatic phone dialing system, would put the receiver up to Annie's ear, and then leave her alone to make the calls. The machine would dial numbers in her local area, and when someone would answer Annie would say something like this:

> Hello, my name is Annie, and I'm a quadriplegic lying in bed. I'm not calling to ask for money, but I would like to tell you the story of my best friend Jesus Christ. Would you please talk to me for a few minutes?

When Annie died a few years later, the man telling this story went to her funeral, which was held at Annie's home in the mountains. When he arrived he had to struggle his way through a huge crowd of people that had gathered all over the property. He asked Annie's family who all the people were, and they said that they were all people that Annie had led to the Lord over the telephone!

Why didn't God take Annie home to Heaven at some time early in her affliction? That's why: hundreds of people were saved as a result of a woman that couldn't even feed or take care of herself. And if you or I ever get in a condition like that, or are in one right now, don't automatically think, or let the Devil tell you, that it is punishment for some sin in your life. Again, that is something you will have to pray about, and something only God can reveal to you. But it may just be that He knows there is still something valuable you can do for the glory and pleasure of God, and the reward for it will be worth all the trouble and heartache you go through.

I recently heard about a young man who was telling people that God gave my pastor leukemia because he was a compromiser. The supposed reason for being a compromiser was because he had built a large church, and this young kid thought that no one could do that if he wasn't soft soaping the word of God and standards. What a child's mentality and lack of understanding of the Bible and true Christian life! According to that kind of thinking, the Apostle Peter must have been a compromiser when three thousand people were saved and became church members in Acts 2. Is that the reason Peter was persecuted and eventually killed, or why his mother-in-law was sick in Matthew 8? Did God make Lazarus sick and allow him to die because he was a compromiser or had some bad sin in his life? No, John 11 tells us that God caused the sickness to show the glory of God! It is more probable that Pastor is afflicted because he is *not* a compromiser.

> 1Pe 2:19-21 *"For this is thankworthy, if a man for conscience toward God endure grief, suffering wrongfully. For what glory is it, if, when ye be buffeted for your faults, ye shall take it patiently?* <u>*but if, when ye do well, and suffer for it, ye take it patiently, this is acceptable with God.*</u> *For even hereunto were ye called: because Christ also suffered for us, leaving us an example, that ye should follow his steps:"*

Sickness and death are not always because of sin in a person's life. Many times it is sent our way because we are *good Christians,* and God can use the trial in our lives to make us even better and bring glory to His Name. Look at the following verse and tell me the death of this child was because of his sin.

1Ki 14:12-13 "Arise thou therefore, get thee to thine own
house: and when thy feet enter into the city, the child shall
die. And all Israel shall mourn for him, and bury him: for he
only of Jeroboam shall come to the grave, <u>because in him there</u>
<u>is found some good thing toward the LORD God of Israel</u> in
the house of Jeroboam."

God took the child because he was good, not evil; if God had allowed him to live, his destiny on earth would most likely have been a life of sin and wickedness because of the influence of his parents.

Brethren, sometimes death or disease is caused by some sin in our lives; and for that reason we must coldly and honestly examine our lives, and pray to see if that is the cause. But don't ever believe someone who tells you God has made you sick because of some sin in your life without you going to the throne of God to find out if it is true or not. The sickness or death of a Christian may be caused by just the opposite. If God has taken a Christian home, it may be because he is a good person, and has suffered enough for His glory, or that He has sent the sickness in order for people to see God's power and glory through him.

One thing I have never been able to understand is why true Born Again Christians, who have been saved by faith in the shed blood of the Lord Jesus Christ, are afraid of death or the Rapture. I understand why lost people are, and should be afraid; their destiny is eternal torment. And I understand Christians from one aspect, that they want more time in order to win people to

Christ; but other than that, I don't understand that thinking.

Many years ago I was attending a Missions Conference in San Antonio, and my roommate, who I will call B____, was a missionary to the Philippines. He and I were praying before the meeting one day, and the end of my prayer was for the Lord to call us home just as soon as possible. When we were finished praying B____ said that he agreed with my prayer except for the last part about wanting the Rapture. He told me that he was having too much fun serving the Lord down here, and didn't want to go home yet! As soon as I heard that I knew that this young man had never been through anything serious in his life. Fun serving the Lord? I have never found much about serving the Lord to be *fun*. Joyful, yes. But "fun," a word that is never even used once in the entire Bible? To me there is something very wrong with a Christian who does not want to go Home to a place of perfect peace, rest, and fellowship with the Lord. There can't be much depth of the knowledge of God in his life.

As I write these lines, I am sitting in a very uncomfortable seat in a twenty-two foot travel trailer 350 miles from my home. My wife, two dachshunds, and I have been here for nine weeks. For all of those nine weeks I have wanted to do one thing – go home. There have been times that I've gotten to the point where I didn't even care if the treatment failed, because I just wanted to go home to a place of comfort and peace. However, even at home there will be a multitude of problems to deal with, and probably more than I have right now. But in Heaven there won't be one single thing to cause discomfort or trouble for as long as God lives!

Why would I want to stay here instead of going there? Fear death? Not a chance, I look forward to it. I may not be too crazy about the *way* I die, but death itself no longer frightens me. Paul said it best in Philippians:

> *Php 1:21-23 "For to me to live is Christ, and to die is gain. But if I live in the flesh, this is the fruit of my labour: yet what I shall choose I wot not. For I am in a strait betwixt two, having a desire to depart, and to be with Christ; which is far better:"*

In Acts 14 Paul was preaching in the city of Lystra; and, because of a rumor, the people rose up and stoned him to death. In Paul's own testimony of the event in 2 Corinthians 12:1-5, he says that he was caught up into Heaven where he saw and heard unspeakable things, the glory of them was so great. And then, after seeing, in person, all the things he had been preaching about for years, the Lord played a dirty trick on Paul, and gave him his life back. Paul woke up bleeding, bruised, and in pain under a pile of rocks. And what was the first thing he did after that? He went right back into Lystra! Why? Any sane man would have left that place as quickly as possible and never gone back. Why did he go back? I think it's pretty obvious that he was trying to get himself stoned and return to Heaven again, probably hoping the Lord would allow him to stay this time. You may say my interpretation of the event is crazy, but is it? Look at Paul's testimony in 1 Corinthians 11:23-28 and tell me a man that lives like that is living carefully. He seems almost suicidal in his approach to serving the Lord.

Why? He knew the Lord in a very real and intimate way, and had seen the glories of Heaven. Who would want to continue living down here after that! What could possibly be better that to go home to God? Brethren, to fear death is to not trust, understand, or believe God. Being sorry for leaving some lost people that are dear to us – certainly, but not for any glory of treasure *this* world has to offer.

My one night in the hospital last year, when I was particularly near death, was a very special time I will never forget. God was very real and close to me that night, and, as I sat watching the clock waiting for death, there was perfect calmness in my heart. I was, indeed, like Paul. My thoughts went to my family and how I didn't want to leave them behind, but there was no fear of the imminent death I was facing. The comfort of the Lord was real, and I would have welcomed His taking me home.

> Ps 23:4 *"Yea, though I walk through the valley of the shadow of death, I will fear no evil: for thou art with me; thy rod and thy staff they comfort me."*

The Comforter had come to me, and to be in the presence of that comfort for eternity was a welcome thought.

Brethren, strive to know God better on a daily basis, and all fear of the unknown, whether death, loss of fortune or fame, abandonment, or other earthly problem will lose the power to make you afraid. Fear of the unknown is a primary factor that keeps people in bondage. They would rather suffer with what they know, than take a chance on what they do not know. But there is no reason for a Christian not to know the future. It is written in the book that God Himself gave for just that purpose. So that we can know God, ourselves, and our future. Those words are true and sure! Brethren, God is in control, and we have nothing to fear.

1Jo 4:17 -18 *"Herein is our love made perfect, that we may have boldness in the day of judgment: because as he is, so are we in this world. There is no fear in love; but perfect love casteth out fear: because fear hath torment. He that feareth is not made perfect in love."*

Let me leave this chapter with the words of one of Bruce Frye's songs called "Heaven Bound."[14]

Don't cry for me, when my life's over,
For my soul, He'll come to claim,
Because I know, I'll live forever,
There within the Lord's domain.

And if I'm there before this day is over,
I'll be there before you know I'm gone,
Don't shed for me those tears of sorrow,
For Jesus takes care of His own.

Don't mourn for me when I have left here,
Eternal peace, there, will be found,
The choice was mine from the beginning,

---

[14] Bruce Frye, *That Was Me,* (Faith Music Missions, Evansville, IN 47728).

My Savior knows I'm Heaven bound.

And if I'm there before this day is over,
I'll be there before you know I'm gone,
Don't shed for me those tears of sorrow,
For Jesus takes care of His own.

Ps 116:15 *"Precious in the sight of the LORD is the death of his saints."*

Chapter Thirteen: Salvation

This book has been written to those who profess to be saved and know the Lord as their personal Savior. There may be, however, those reading this that are not sure of their salvation, or who have never come to a saving knowledge of, and a personal relationship with, the Lord Jesus Christ. This chapter is written to you that you may know Him Who knows everything about you. The Bible states that *"God is not willing that any should perish..."* (2 Peter 3:9). In John 3:16 you will read just how much God loves you, and how much it cost Him to have you in Heaven with Him. His love is beyond human comprehension. He gave His only begotten Son, to live the sinless life you could not live, to be tortured to the point of almost being unrecognizable (Isaiah 52:14), to die a horrible death on the cross to pay for your sin, and to rise from the dead so that one day you could do the same, and be with Him in Heaven. And He makes all of this a free gift to "whosoever will." But you must also understand that God's mercy does have a limit. If you turn away from this gift; if you turn your back on God and His mercy now, then you will have no mercy for all eternity. Dear friend, you are not waiting for judgment; that has already taken place the moment you became old enough to become accountable for your sins. You are merely waiting for final sentencing.

> Jn 3:36 *"He that believeth on the Son hath everlasting life: and he that believeth not the Son shall not see life; but the wrath of God abideth on him."*

As I have already stated, the love of God is beyond our comprehension, but so too is the wrath of God.

> *Luke 16.23 "And in hell he lift up his eyes, being in torments, and seeth Abraham afar off, and Lazarus in his bosom."*

Please understand that it is not God's will for you to die and burn forever. But if you refuse the righteousness offered to you freely, by the blood sacrifice of the Lord Jesus Christ, and shun God's offer, He is perfectly justified as your Creator to do with you whatever He wishes. You can be made clean by the forgiveness of sins through accepting the payment Jesus Christ made for you, or you can be kept from infecting anyone ever again, and pay for your own sins, in the purifying fires of Hell. When I was a child and got a splinter in my finger, my mother would take a needle and dig the splinter out. However, the first thing she did was to purify the needle in fire. The reason for that was that there was nothing in that fire that could infect me. The fire was pure.

The decision between heaven or hell is completely your choice, God does not and will not make that decision for you.

> *Re 22:17 "And the Spirit and the bride say, Come. And let him that heareth say, Come. And let him that is athirst come. And <u>whosoever will</u>, let him take the water of life <u>freely</u>."*

Please read and pray about the following information, as the true doctrine of salvation is your only hope for Heaven.

If the Bible is very clear and specific about anything, it is clear about the doctrine of salvation. Now, you may argue with me on that point because of the multitude of religions in the world, many of which have a different plan of salvation other than the New Testament one of salvation by grace through faith in the shed blood of the Lord Jesus Christ. And many of these false teachings actually come from the Bible itself because of the inability, or unwillingness, of people to study and divide the Bible correctly. Notice what the Apostle Paul said to the young preacher Timothy in 2 Tim 2.15.

"Study to shew thyself approved unto God, a workman that needeth not to be ashamed, rightly dividing the word of truth."

In order to understand the Bible, we must see that there are divisions in the scripture. Some of them apply to us doctrinally and some don't. There are several applications of any passage of scripture. A passage can be for doctrine, practical living, history, or for a spiritual application. In addition, some of the Bible is written to the people of the Old Testament, some of it to the people of the New Testament, and some of it to the people of the Tribulation and Millennium which are yet in the future. This subject is called "dispensations." Many people may *read* the Bible, but not many do as the commandment says – *study and rightly divide it.* Every false Bible doctrine comes from simply taking a passage of scripture, and building a doctrine on it without regard to who or when the passage applies, or by adding to the Bible something that it does not say, or taking out of the Bible something it does say. And that is where many of the Bible "contradictions" come from.

After being a Bible student for almost thirty-one years, graduating from Bible Institute where I studied the Bible in both Hebrew and Greek, and studying the supposed contradictions, let me make this definitive statement. There are no errors, mistakes, or contradictions of any kind in the King James Authorized Bible. It is the pure, preserved, word of God. Through all the ages and languages it has been preserved for us by God's own hand; we can read it, and put our faith in it, with the absolute confidence that we are reading exactly what God wants us to have. Don't let anyone tell you that you need some Hebrew or Greek manuscript in order for you to know what the Bible really says. That is a game that con-men play in order to take away the authority of the scripture and put it on themselves. After all, do you speak, read, or write Hebrew or Greek? Well then, you must put your faith in Dr. ____ and his P.H.D. in order to know the truth, right? Absolutely not. Go buy yourself an Authorized King James Bible, and you'll have exactly what you need: the living Word of the living God.

But this is not a book on the authority of the scriptures. If you wish to study that subject, please go online to www.daystarpublishing.org, and search for books and tracts on the subject.

But the doctrine of salvation, by grace through faith, is found all through the Pauline epistles. It is the primary theme of the books of Romans and Galatians in particular. Even a cursory reading of Romans 7 will show that God has made salvation just as easy for us as He possibly could. God proved to man through the thousands of years of the Old Testament that man could not keep the Law of God the way he was commanded. Man failed time and time and time again, and that is why God made the provision for the forgiveness of man's sin through the sacrifice of a lamb. But an animal was not a perfect substitute, as Hebrews 9 and 10 show us. Sins were "forgiven" in the Old Testament, but not "taken away." They were not cleared. Enter the Lord Jesus Christ on earth, and we see John the Baptist making this statement:

Jn 1:29 "The next day John seeth Jesus coming unto him, and saith, Behold the <u>Lamb</u> *of God, which* <u>taketh away</u> *the sin of the world."*

God sent Jesus Christ, His Son, not only so that our sins could be forgiven, but also so that they could be cleared from the record completely, and we could stand before God guiltless. Good works have nothing to do with it. If you think they do, please ask yourself this question: If I can earn my own way to Heaven by doing good things, why did Jesus Christ have to be my sacrifice for sins? Please understand this, Jesus Christ already paid for our sins, so there is nothing left for us to pay! And God will not accept your attempts to pay it by your own self-righteous works.

Let me illustrate it this way: Let's say you owed a great debt you could not pay to a local store owner or credit card company. They were demanding payment, but you couldn't pay all that you owed. Then you met me and told me of your troubles. I made the offer to pay your debt for you without expecting any payment to myself in return. I go to your debtor and pay the debt in full; you now owe nothing. Now you have a choice to make. You can either accept my gift of "salvation," or you can refuse it and try to make payments on the debt that is already paid, still trying to justify yourself by your own good works. Those are the only two choices you have. Now let me ask you this. If the debt had been paid by me, and the entity you owed the money to was honest, would they accept your attempts to make payments? No, of course not. The debt was already paid. You *cannot* make a payment, it will *not* be accepted. Your offer will be refused!

In the same way, God will not accept any attempts of yours to pay a debt that has already been paid by His Son. All He expects you to do is accept the payment made in your behalf. You owe Him nothing in return. You may ask at this point why we say that you should live your life serving God? You live it as an obedient child would follow his father's wishes, but not as someone trying to become part of the family. Notice Ephesians 2 again:

Eph 2:8-9 "For by grace are ye saved through faith; and that not of yourselves: it is the gift of God: Not of works, lest any man should boast."

What could be more simple? If I offered you a Christmas gift, would you have to pay for it? Of course not; what kind of gift would that be! No, all you have to do is reach out and accept it. And would I be offended if you refused my offer? Yes, I certainly would. Look at it again in Titus 3:

Tit 3:5-6 "<u>Not by works of righteousness which we have done</u>, but according to his mercy he saved us, by the washing of regeneration, and renewing of the Holy Ghost; Which he shed on us abundantly through Jesus Christ our Saviour;"

So how then do you accept the gift of God? It is almost too simple, but that was exactly what God designed it to be – simple. So simple that someone living in a grass hut in the jungle, or a scientist working on a cure for cancer, could understand it.

1. You must admit that you are a sinner and are not worthy of God's mercy:

Ro 3:23 "For all have sinned, and come short of the glory of God;"

Ro 5:8 "But God commendeth his love toward us, in that, while we were yet sinners, Christ died for us."

2. You must admit your own righteousness is not good enough to save you:

Ro 3:10 "As it is written, There is none righteous, no, not one:"

3. You must admit that the Lord Jesus Christ is the *only* Savior:

Ac 4:10 "Be it known unto you all, and to all the people of Israel, that by the name of Jesus Christ of Nazareth, whom ye crucified, whom God raised from the dead, even by him doth this man stand here before you whole."

Ac 4:12 "Neither is there salvation in any other: for there is none other name under heaven given among men, whereby we must be saved."

Jn 14:6 "Jesus saith unto him, I am the way, the truth, and the life: no man cometh unto the Father, but by me."

4. You must accept Him as your personal Savior and ask Him to save you.

Jn 1:12 "But as many as received him, to them gave he power to become the sons of God, even to them that believe on his name:"

Ro 10:8 -13 "But what saith it? The word is nigh thee, even in thy mouth, and in thy heart: that is, the word of faith, which we preach; That if thou shalt confess with thy mouth the Lord Jesus, and shalt believe in thine heart that God hath raised him from the dead, thou shalt be saved. For with the heart man believeth unto righteousness; and with the mouth confession is made unto salvation. For the scripture saith, Whosoever believeth on him shall not be ashamed. For there is no difference between the Jew and the Greek: for the same Lord over all is rich unto all that call upon him. For whosoever shall call upon the name of the Lord shall be saved."

5. Rest in what God has done for you.

Mt 11:28 "Come unto me, all ye that labour and are heavy laden, and I will give you rest."

Here is a simple prayer for you to pray in order to be saved. Please realize it is not by reciting a prayer that you are saved, but by your heart reaching out to a Holy God and trusting on His mercy.

Dear Jesus,
I believe in my heart that you are the one true and living God. I believe that you died in my place to pay for all my sins, and that you rose again the third day. I confess to you that I am a sinner and not worthy of your mercy. Right now I ask you to forgive my sins, and wash them away by the blood the Lord Jesus Christ shed for me. I receive you as my personal Savior by faith, and ask you to save my soul from destruction and Hell. I put my trust in you, and you only, for my salvation, and ask you

to take me to Heaven someday. I accept your free gift of eternal life, and ask you to fill and seal me with the Holy Ghost. Thank you for dying for me, and for saving my soul. Amen.

If you have done these things, and truly put all your faith and confidence in Jesus Christ by faith alone, then you no longer need worry about your eternal destiny. God will not break His promise to you *ever*, for any reason. You are saved now and forever, and are a member of the Family of God.

If you have made this decision in your life and have asked the Lord to save you, or have other questions about this subject, please write to me at the following address:

Bob Murphy
C/O Treasure Valley Baptist Church
1300 S. Teare Ave.
Meridian, ID 83642

I would also suggest reading a book called *Done* by Cary Schmidt[15] if you would like the most simple and complete explanation of the gospel I have ever read. It is a small, easy to read book that costs only about $3.00. You can order it from the Treasure Valley Baptist Church Bookstore at the above address, or order it directly from "Striving Together" at www.strivingtogether.com.

---

[15] Cary Schmidt, *Done,* (Striving Together Publications: Lancaster, CA, 2005).

Chapter Fourteen: Conclusion

Here are just a few more thoughts as we conclude this book, that were a blessing to me, and I hope will be the same for you.

1000 Marbles

The older I get, the more I enjoy Saturday mornings. Perhaps it's the quiet solitude that comes with being the first to rise, or maybe it's the unbounded joy of not having to be at work. Either way, the first few hours of a Saturday morning are the most enjoyable.

A few weeks ago, I was shuffling toward the garage with a steaming cup of coffee in one hand and the morning paper in the other. What began as a typical Saturday morning turned into one of those lessons that life seems to hand you from time to time. Let me tell you about it.

I turned the dial up into the phone portion of the band on my ham radio in order to listen to a Saturday morning swap net. Along the way, I came across an older sounding chap, with a tremendous signal and a golden voice. You know the kind; he sounded like he should be in the broadcasting business. He was telling whom-ever he was talking with something about "a thousand marbles." I was intrigued and stopped to listen to what he had to say: "Well, Tom, it sure sounds like you're busy with your job. I'm sure they pay you well but it's a shame you have to be away from home and your family so much. Hard to believe a young fellow should have to work sixty or seventy hours a week to make ends meet. It's too bad you missed your daughter's dance recital" he continued.

"Let me tell you something that has helped me keep my own priorities." And that's when he began to explain his theory of a "thousand marbles."

"You see, I sat down one day and did a little arithmetic. The average person lives about seventy-five years. I know, some live more and some live less, but on average, folks live about seventy-five years. "Now then, I multiplied 75 times 52 and I came up with 3900, which is the number of Saturdays that the average person has in their entire lifetime. Now, stick with me, Tom, I'm getting to the important part.

It took me until I was fifty-five years old to think about all this in any detail," he went on, "and by that time I had lived through over twenty-eight hundred Saturdays." "I got to thinking that if I lived to be seventy-five, I only had about a thousand of them left to enjoy. So I went to a toy store and bought every single marble they had. I ended up having to visit three toy stores to round up 1000 marbles. I took them home and put them inside a large, clear plastic container right here in the shack next to my gear."

"Every Saturday since then, I have taken one marble out and thrown it away. I found that by watching the marbles diminish, I focused more on the really important things in life. There is nothing like watching your time here on this earth run out to help get your priorities straight."

"Now let me tell you one last thing before I sign-off with you and take my lovely wife out for breakfast. This morning, I took the very last marble out of the container. I figure that if I make it until next Saturday then I have been given a little extra time. And the one thing we can all use is a little more time."

You could have heard a pin drop on the band when this fellow signed off. I guess he gave us all a lot to think about. I had planned to work on the antenna that morning, and then I was going to meet up with a few hams to work on the next club newsletter. Instead, I went upstairs and woke my wife up with a kiss. "C'mon honey, I'm taking you and the kids to breakfast." "What brought this on?" she asked with a smile. "Oh, nothing special, it's just been a long time since we spent a Saturday together with the kids. And hey, can we stop at a toy store while we're out? I need to buy some marbles.

Anonymous

And so, dear reader, may I ask what your priorities in life are? If you suffer from chronic illness, and the Lord allows you to spend more time on earth, what will you do with that time? I have shown you the purpose of life found in Revelation 4:11. Even if you are bedridden, you are not useless in God's eyes. You can pray like very few people can. You can use the phone to call and encourage others, or even dial at random and witness to people over the phone. Send a letter to your local prison or county jail and address it to "Any Inmate." You will be surprised where those letters will end up. Perhaps you could even teach a class at your bedside showing others the things you have learned. Rest assured, you have not suffered in vain. God has a purpose for you, and your joy will be in finding out and accomplishing that purpose. Your other choice is to sit or lie there complaining of your mistreatment and misfortune; the choice is once again all yours. I hope God will give you the grace to make the right choice.

In John 6 we find a small boy who brought his lunch to Jesus as a gift. It was a poor boy's meal of a couple of small fish and a loaf of barley bread (the cheapest kind of bread available). And what did Jesus do with it? Did He refuse it because it wasn't a worthy gift? No, He accepted it. But then, He broke the bread. Only then was there enough to distribute to the masses. God will always break what is offered to him. He breaks what he takes, then blesses and uses it to meet men's needs. Isn't that what you've seen happen in Christian lives all around you, or of ones you've read about somewhere? You give yourself to the Lord, and at once everything goes so badly wrong that you are tempted to find fault with His ways. To persist in such fault finding will cause the will to be broken. Yes indeed, but to what purpose? It will break your will, but will also break your spirit. You have gone too far for the world to use you, but you have not gone far enough for God. This is the tragedy of many a Christian. Do we want Him to use us? Then our will must be broken, but not our spirit. Day by day let us go on giving to Him, not finding fault with His methods, but accepting His handling of us with praise and expectation. And remember also, that little boy in John 6 went home with far more than he gave to the Lord. I'll guarantee you that at least one, if not all of those baskets of fragments that were left went to that boy!

Here is another example of someone was given wholly to the cause of Christ:

In 1980 a young man from Rwanda was forced by his tribe to either renounce Christ or face certain death. He refused to renounce Christ, and he was killed on the spot. The night before he had written the following commitment which was found in his room:

164

"I'm part of the fellowship of the unashamed, the die has been cast, I have stepped over the line, the decision has been made - I'm a disciple of Jesus Christ. I won't look back, let up, slow down, back away or be still.

My past is redeemed, my present makes sense, my future is secure. I'm finished and done with low living, sight walking, smooth knees, colorless dreams, tamed vision, worldly talking, cheap giving & dwarfed goals.

My face is set, my gait is fast, my goal is Heaven, the road is narrow, my way is rough, my companions are few, my guide is reliable, my mission is clear. I won't give up, shut up, let up until I have stayed up, stored up, prayed up for the cause of Jesus Christ.

I must go till He comes, give till I drop, preach till everyone knows, work till He stops me & when He comes for His own, He will have no trouble recognizing me because my banner will have been clear."[16]

By Dr. Bob Moorehead

And one more for those we love and leave behind.

"If tomorrow starts without me,
And I'm not there to see,
If the sun should rise and find your eyes all filled with tears for me;
I wish so much you wouldn't cry the way you did today,
While thinking of the many things,
We didn't get to say.
I know how much you love me,
As much as I love you,
And each time that you think of me, I know you'll miss me too;

---

[16] Source unknown.

But when tomorrow starts without me,
Please try to understand,
That an angel came and called my name,
And took me by the hand,
And said my place was ready,
In Heaven far above,
And that I'd have to leave behind all those I dearly
love.
But as I turned to walk away,
A tear fell from my eye,
For all my life, I'd always thought, I didn't want to die.
I had so much to live for,
So much left yet to do,
It seemed almost impossible, that I was leaving you. I
thought of all the yesterdays,
The good ones and the bad,
I thought of all that we have shared,
And all the fun we had.
If I could relive yesterday,
Just even for a while,
I'd say good-bye and kiss you and maybe see you
smile.
But then I fully realized,
That this could never be,
For emptiness and memories, would take the place of
me.
And when I thought of worldly things, that I might
miss tomorrow,
I thought of you, and when I did, My heart was filled
with sorrow.
But when I walked through Heaven's gates,
I felt so much at home.
When God looked down and smiled at me,
From His great golden throne,
He said, 'This is eternity, And all I've promised you.'

Today your life on earth is past, but here life starts anew.
I promise no tomorrow,
But today will always last,
And since each day is the same way,
There's no longing for the past.'
So when tomorrow starts without me, don't think we're far apart,
For every time you think of me, I'm right here, in your heart"

I hope this book has been a blessing to you; it was certainly meant to be so. The Fight For Light is the most difficult battle any Christian will ever undertake. May God richly bless you in whatever His plans may be. One day we will all be able to sit next to the banks of the river and stare at the glories of God and New Jerusalem. How insignificant our problems down here will seem to us then. "Life on earth is a life of trust; life in Heaven is a life of understanding." Someday the purpose of all our trials and sufferings will be revealed. Until then, all we have is trust; let us not allow it to fail.

Bob Murphy
September 2012
A Trophy of God's Grace

Chapter Fifteen: Epilog

September 2012 - As I am putting the finishing touches on this book, some new developments have taken place in my own health situation. As I've stated, I've had this disease for thirty-five years and have fought several battles in the last three years as a result. But now we see the real possibility of a God-given victory. After eight weeks of the new treatment, we are further down the road toward full recovery that we were after seven months of the old treatment. Last year my viral count started off at seventy million and dropped to one hundred thirty three thousand before the virus mutated and the treatment failed. This year my count started at fifty million, and after eight weeks it is down to nineteen thousand! Unless something once again goes wrong, in another few weeks the virus will be dead. I am once again at home in Boise, ID, looking forward to God's plan for my future. To God be all the glory! Yes, medical science has its share of the victory; but only because God enabled them to find and use the cure. My sincere thanks to all those in the medical community for their help and sacrifice in the behalf of others, and to the multitude of Christians that prayed and supported us all through this trial; but, most importantly, my eternal love and thanks go to God my Savior. May the life you have returned to me be ever pleasing to Thee! Amen.

November 2012 – Just before going to print, some new developments have once again occurred. As I said above, by this time the virus should have been dead. Just as in January, when we expected a call from the doctor saying we had won, she instead called and said the virus had won. A few weeks ago we were again waiting for the same call announcing that we had won. Instead, however, the doctor called and announced my viral count had once again risen. It has continued to rise, and the doctors have now stopped this latest treatment. Medical science has run its course. My doctor says I should have one to five years to live, but I am convinced that God gave me a promise, several months ago, that I am going to live. So that is where our faith rests. Is it God, the Devil, or just a really nasty disease that continues to frustrate us all? The answer is, that it doesn't really matter. What is important is how Pam and I react to it, and what we do about it. However, last night I believe the Lord did something special for me, that heralds back to chapter six of this book. I believe God showed me the answer to "why."

For quite some time, the Lord has impressed on me that His will, at this time, is for me to write books. How many, one or twenty, I have no idea. There is, however, a problem with that for me. All of my life I have lived outdoors; I have never liked being cooped up in a room, and especially not sitting at a desk studying. When I was in high school, I was faster than any tract sprinter on our high school team when it came time for the last bell of the day to ring. I was out the door like a blur. Grade school and college were the same. The walls were closing in on me and I had to get outside.

On a recent Friday night, after I had taken my medication injections, I sat staring at the empty syringes, and the Lord spoke to my heart. The thought came to me that there was no way I would be sitting still, writing a book, if God hadn't taken every other possibility of doing something else away from me. It is no longer possible for me to live my life outdoors. At this time, I can't even stand on my feet for more than a few minutes without becoming completely fatigued. There is only one thing I can do right now, and that is to sit! My choices now are either to become a couch potato, sitting and wasting time watching TV; or, to be useful for Christ and sit at a desk studying and writing. Which do you think is the better choice? So here I sit, living a life that, a year ago, I never would have even considered. I'm writing a book that I hope will be a blessing to others and to the Lord. I am faced with the fact that if God wants me to continue writing, He may never heal me. No matter what I try to promise the Lord about continuing to write, even if He does heal me, I think He and I both know me well enough to realize that the day He heals me, I will once again be out the door like greased lightning! I am faced with "...*not my will but thine be done.*" That is the Christian Life, and to think or hope any differently is only self-delusion. Attitude, once again, is the all-important factor here. To love, trust, and follow the Lord when His will goes perpendicular to my will! Brethren, that IS the cross we all must bear. Once again, the correct decision is: "No surrender" to the enemies of God. May it always, by the grace of God, be my theme and yours.

2Th 1:4-5 "So that we ourselves glory in you in the churches of God for your patience and faith in all your persecutions and tribulations that ye endure: Which is a manifest token of the righteous judgment of God, that ye may be counted worthy of the kingdom of God, for which ye also suffer:"

> Ps 112:7 "He shall not be afraid of evil tidings: his heart is fixed, trusting in the LORD."

Nu 6:24 -26 "The LORD bless thee, and keep thee: The LORD make his face shine upon thee, and be gracious unto thee: The LORD lift up his countenance upon thee, and give thee peace."

Recommended Reading

Dr. Sam Gipp, *Living With Pain,* (Daystar Publishing Inc., P.O. Box 464, Miamitown, OH, 45041, www.daystarpublishing.org)

Henry Frost, *Miraculous Healing,* (Christian Focus Publications Ltd., www.christianfocus.com,)

Joni Eareckson Tada, *The God I Love,* (Zondervan, Grand Rapids, MI, 49530, www.zondervan.com)

Index